Managing Editor
Karen J. Goldfluss, M.S. Ed.

Editor-in-Chief
Sharon Coan, M.S. Ed.

Illustrator
Renee Christine Yates

Cover Artist
Brenda DiAntonis

Art Coordinator
Kevin Barnes

Art Director
CJae Froshay

Imaging
Ralph Olmedo, Jr.
James Edward Grace

Product Manager
Phil Garcia

Publishers
Rachelle Cracchiolo, M.S. Ed.
Mary Dupuy Smith, M.S. Ed.

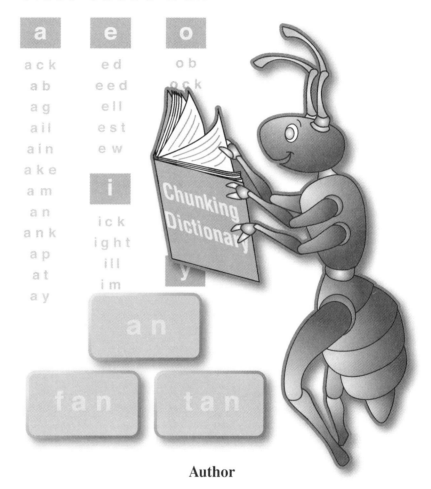

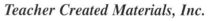

Author

Carol Kirkham Martin

Teacher Created Materials, Inc.
6421 Industry Way
Westminster, CA 92683
www.teachercreated.com.
ISBN-0-7439-3287-0
©2003 Teacher Created Materials, Inc.
Made in U.S.A.

Table of Contents

Introduction

▼◀▲▼◀▲▼◀▲▼◀▲▼◀▲▼◀▲▼◀▲▼◀▲▼▶▲▼▶▲▼▶▲▼▶▲▼

Why Use Word Chunks?

Studies have shown that children can read, spell, and comprehend more effectively when they look for familiar parts of words instead of sounding them out one letter at a time.

As adult readers, we automatically look for familiar groups of letters when we encounter a new word. Sounding out each letter takes too long and all the rules and exceptions interfere with fluency. Our students need to read smoothly to gain meaning from print. They need to be taught chunking, the efficient process used by strong adult readers.

Teaching onsets, or beginning sounds, digraphs, and blends is something we have done for years. However, we also need to teach children the sound for the chunk—the vowel and letters that follow. In the past we tried building charts of word families with students, but children didn't always transfer this new knowledge to reading, writing, and spelling. Many children also had difficulty recalling the sound for each chunk, especially during independent practice. *Word Chunks* provides visual cues, student reference materials, and hands-on manipulative activities. It uses these materials to give students many opportunities to interact with each chunk and make chunking an accessible tool.

Word Chunks includes hands-on activities to allow students to connect chunking with reading, writing, and spelling. Use as many activities as your learners require. However, keep in mind that chunking is only one part of teaching reading. Children need to travel with a grab bag of strategies for predicting new words. Furthermore, it is important to balance instruction between strategies and comprehension to ensure that our learners become successful readers.

Which Chunks Should You Introduce?

If you teach the chunks your students will meet most often, you will give them a valuable tool. In 1998, Edward Fry suggested teaching the 38 most-commonly used chunks (Janiel Wagstaff, *Teaching Reading and Writing With Word Walls*, page 68; original source—*The Reading Teacher*, 1998, p.61). They are listed below and used in this text.

ab	ank	ew	ink	ow
ack	ap	ick	ip	uck
ag	at	ight	ob	ug
ail	ay	ill	ock	um
ain	ed	im	op	unk
ake	eed	in	ore	y
am	ell	ine	ot	
an	est	ing	out	

Getting Started

Organizing Your Chunking Materials

As teachers, you have many demands made on your time, so parents and volunteers are an important resource. Train them to use office equipment and keep instructions for ongoing projects and a box of supplies in a central location so it is readily available when they come into the room to help. This text will remind you to seek volunteer help with appropriate projects to lighten your load.

Ask volunteers to make a folder for each chunk. Even before the students arrive, let your helpers make a copy of the reproducible pages in this book. Store them in the corresponding folder for each chunk. They can also make a Chunking Computer for each child by following the assembly directions included on page 9. This is also a good time for them to enlarge, copy, and laminate the Chunking Contest Poster on page 63. (Prior to copying, fill in the blanks with your own details.)

As you find poems and simple books to introduce or practice a chunk, make a copy or list the title on the corresponding file folder. When your students are ready to start chunking, you will simply select the folder for the chunk you have chosen and begin teaching.

Organizing Students' Chunking Materials

Ask each child to bring in a two-pocket folder with brads. This request can be included on a supply list sent home to parents at the beginning of the school year. Write each child's name on the front of his or her folder. Copy the Student Word Chunks (pages 56–60), punch them with a three-hole punch, and put them in the brads of the folder. The pockets of the folder will be used to store the Chunking Computer and, if needed, chunking flash cards.

Using the Chunk Cards

Reproduce the chunk cards from the back of this book (pages 72–91). To ensure durability, laminate these cards before you begin using them. If you have a magnetic chalk board, attach a magnetic strip to the back of each card. This will allow you to move the card from the chalkboard to the bulletin board and back again as you teach. Choose bulletin board space close to the area you will use for reading instruction. Staple the title, "Chunk Wall" (page 72) at the top of the board and add letters for the five vowels and **y** directly beneath. After you have taught a chunk, use a pushpin to hang the card under its beginning vowel on the chunk wall. (Note: A pocket chart can be used instead of a bulletin board, if preferred.)

Getting Started (cont.)

Beginning Chunking

The hard-to-break habit of sounding out each letter can slow down reading and thereby inhibit comprehension. For this reason, students need good reading habits right from the beginning. Prepare learners for chunking by engaging them in listening games to develop sound discrimination. The following sequenced list of activities will help them hear sounds needed for reading and spelling:

- Practice discrimination of words. Ask, "Are these words the same? cat—cat, cow—cow, horse—sheep."
- Practice discrimination of beginning sounds. Ask, "Do these words start with the same sound? cow—cat, horse—chicken, pig—picture."
- Practice discrimination of ending sounds. Ask, "Do these words end with the same sound? dog—pig, car—four, book—crayon."
- Practice discrimination of rhyming words. Ask, "Do these words rhyme? Do they sound the same in the middle and end? cat—hat, log—hog, door—barn."

When students perceive a match, ask them to signal their response in a fun way, such as clapping, flashing a self-made smiley card, or using a body movement such as thumbs up. Vary the activity and response to make practice fun.

If your students have difficulty hearing the differences in sounds, help them become aware of the position of their mouth as they make the sound. Ask, "How does your tongue/lip/throat move when you start/end that word? Does your mouth move the same way when you start/end these words?" Work through the levels of discrimination until they can consistently notice the difference.

Once the group is able to discriminate sounds, they are ready to connect the letters that make the sound. You can begin by teaching the sound for each letter. Chunking can begin when a child knows about half of the letter sounds.

Choosing a Chunk

To choose the chunk for the week, keep a pad handy and jot down chunks missed by many students during reading, writing, and/or independent work. Select a chunk that will help students move forward with current learning. In this way new knowledge will be transferred easily into past learning to help it become an accessible tool.

If you are working with beginning readers who need to learn everything, begin with a simple chunk such as /**at**/. You will see this chunk modeled throughout the text.

Daily Plans for the Week

▼◄▲▼◄▲▼◄▲▼◄▲▼◄▲▼◄▲▼◄▲▼◄▲▼◄▲▼►▲▼►▲▼►▲▼►▲▼

Monday

Introducing the Idea of Chunking

Explain to your group that they will be learning about chunks, the parts of words that combine with beginning sounds to make words. Tell them learning this way will make reading, writing, and spelling easier and faster.

Introduce the chunk of the week in the context of a piece of meaningful print to enable children to transfer chunking into authentic reading, writing, and spelling. In the beginning, a poem or part of a student-read story, containing the chunk, works well. See the words on pages 72–91 to get you started in your search. (A blank card on page 91 is provided for additional chunks you may wish to introduce.)

As children learn more about reading and writing, you may choose to use samples of their writing to introduce a chunk. Choose a piece of writing of average quality for the group. Be sure to obtain the student's permission ahead of time. Make students feel proud that they are sharing their writing and helping the class learn. Post the enlarged writing sample, passage from a story, or poem near the chunk. You may need to gather the class on the floor in front of the display or use an overhead projector, depending on your teaching situation.

Students need to connect the sound for each chunk with the letters that make that sound. We know that children remember best if instruction engages more than one of the five senses. With this in mind, display the chunk card on the magnetic board (or pocket chart) as you introduce its sound. After you introduce a chunk, bring the chunk card into instruction whenever it appears in other subject areas until the class knows it. This will help children integrate this new knowledge into other learning.

Finding the Sound for the Chunk

Show your group the /at/ card (page 77). (The /at/ chunk is used as an example.) Ask them to name the picture (cat). Cover the onset /c/ and ask students to say just the ending chunk. If some have difficulty, remind them to start with the sound for the vowel and move to the end of the chunk.

When most students respond correctly, ask them to repeat the sound, /at/, as they trace the letters in the air, on the carpet, or on their desks. This allows them to involve their sense of touch and body movement in learning. Do it again, but ask them to spell the chunk as they trace the letters. Refer to the chunk card as they spell to aid memory through the use of a visual.

Daily Plans for the Week (cont.)

▼◀▲▼◀▲▼◀▲▼◀▲▼◀▲▼◀▲▼◀▲▼◀▲▼◀▲▼◀▲▼▶▲▼▶▲▼▶▲▼

Monday (cont.)

Using the Chunks to Read

Challenge students to look for the chunk in the sample or poem you have displayed on a board or pocket chart. Cover the discovered chunks with highlighter tape or highlight them with a light colored marker or crayon. Point to each word containing the chunk and ask the class to give the beginning sound and add the chunk to read the new word. Next, read the entire sample with the class. Students can read the words they know and repeat unfamiliar words after you. With their new knowledge of the chunk, everyone should be able to read some of the words.

Return to the chunk, /**at**/, and again ask students for the sound. Did you hear more correct responses this time? You are already making a difference in their learning.

Using Chunking Throughout the Day

Remind the class that /**at**/ will be the chunk of the week. The chunk card will stay on the front board to help them remember the sound until next Monday when it will become a part of the chunk wall.

Pass out the two-pocket folders containing the Student Word Chunk pages (See page 4). Discuss the grouping of chunks on the chunk wall by beginning vowel sound to enable students to use the chunk wall independently

in the future. Ask them to find the chunk of the week and highlight it with a yellow crayon. Remind students to use this chunk wall whenever they need to spell a word containing the /**at**/ sound. As each additional chunk is learned, revisit the student chunk card for highlighting, letting students practice reference skills as they search on their own for the chunk and highlight it.

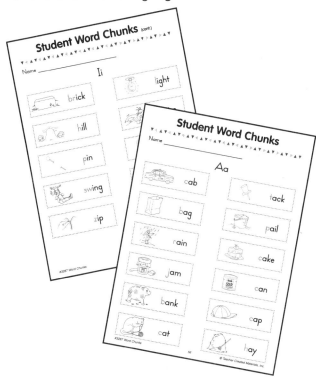

To help children incorporate chunking into their learning throughout the school day, ask them to point out the chunk whenever they notice it. When someone sees the chunk, ask him or her to get the chunk card, check the spelling, and challenge the class to combine the beginning sound with the chunk to read the new word. Soon they will be pointing out chunks in places you never noticed.

Daily Plans for the Week (cont.)

▼◄▲▼◄▲▼◄▲▼◄▲▼◄▲▼◄▲▼◄▲▼◄▲▼◄▲▼►▲▼►▲▼►▲▼►▲▼

Tuesday

Listening for the Chunks

Choose a story or poem that contains the chunk of the week. You can check books listed on page 96. If you are unable to find something suitable, make a list of words including some that contain the chunk and some that do not.

Now you are ready to play "Howdy," a listening game. As you read the poem, story, or list, ask students to signal when they hear the chunk. They can let you know by waving, "Howdy." This activity will give you a chance to assess who is able to hear the sound for the chunk and who needs extra help from an aide, volunteer, or small-group reteaching situation.

Making a Class Chunking Dictionary

Bind 39 sheets of 12" x 18" (30 cm x 46 cm) heavy white drawing paper to make a book.

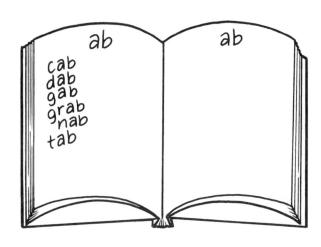

(You may want to add a backing of heavy cardboard to make turning the pages easier. Write "Class Chunking Dictionary" on the first page. This will be the cover page. On the inside of the cover, write the first chunk, /**ab**/. You will use both this page and the one facing it for this chunk. You will write words that contain the chunk on the left side, and the right side will become a picture dictionary made by the students.

Tell the class you will be making a class dictionary of words containing the chunks, but you need their help. Ask students to tell you any words they remember that contain the chunk of the week. These might be words from the poem, story, list, or other words they know from life experience. As a child recalls a word, write it on the left-hand page for that chunk, but let the class tell you how to spell it. Ask questions such as, "Who knows the beginning sound for that word? Who can spell the chunk to finish that word?"

Verbalize what you are thinking as you write each new or irregular spelling. For example, if a child says "chat", you might say, "Chat starts with a sound we haven't learned yet. The sound /**ch**/ is made with the letters **ch**. Who can tell us how to finish writing the word 'chat'?"

Daily Plans for the Week (cont.)

▼◄ ▲▼◄ ▲▼◄ ▲▼◄ ▲▼◄ ▲▼◄ ▲▼◄ ▲▼◄ ▲▼► ▲▼► ▲▼► ▲▼► ▲▼

Tuesday (cont.)

The Chunking Computer

Ask volunteers to copy the chunking computer (page 16) onto card stock or tag board. Make one computer for each child. If you are unable to run tag in your copier this activity can be done with paper computers. However, paper chunking computers may need to be periodically replaced. Another alternative is to glue the paper to tag. (If you use the gluing method, be sure to use a glue stick and put lots of glue around the printer pattern.)

Follow these steps to assemble the computers:

1. Make copies of pages 17–35 and cut along the gray boxes of all the cards. Each week, students will use the word strips to practice their word chunks. Laminate all cards if possible.

2. Use scissors or a craft knife to cut around the bold dashed lines (outer rectangular box) of the pattern on page 16.

3. To prepare the computer, use a craft knife or scissors to cut along the solid dark line (around three sides of the "paper" in the printer), as indicated.

4. Fold back along the dashed lines above and below the computer. Join the edges with a piece of tape to make a slide for the word-picture strip.

5. Put each student's name on the back of his or her "computer."

step 2   step 3

step 4   step 5

Ask students to slide their strips into their "computers", using the right side opening, and resting the strip along the bottom fold as they slide it. They will need to slide the strip until the first word appears on the computer "screen." Ask them to read the word using the beginning sound and the chunk they learned. Call on a student to say the new word. Ask children to gently lift the paper in the printer to see if they are correct. The picture should correspond with the word being read.

This activity can be assigned for individual independent practice or you may want to select pairs of students to practice reading their new words as buddies. Ask students to store their "computer" and word strips in the pocket of their folder for future practice.

         #3287 Word Chunks

Daily Plans for the Week (cont.)

▼◀▲▼◀▲▼◀▲▼◀▲▼◀▲▼◀▲▼◀▲▼◀▲▼▶▲▼▶▲▼▶▲▼▶▲▼

Wednesday

Using Beginning Sounds and Chunks to Make New Words

Now it is time to let your learners test their chunking wings with an independent activity. Review the sound for the chunk of the week. (The /**at**/ chunk will again be used here as an example.) Write the key word *cat,* under the chunk card, hanging on the chalkboard. Explain that you will make a new word by changing the beginning sound. Erase the letter **c** and write **f**. Ask the group to combine the beginning sound with the chunk. Challenge them with the question, "Does that sound like a word you know?" Continue practicing in this way using other letters that can combine with /**at**/ to make real words. Continue until they seem to have the idea.

Pass out copies of the half-page, "Word Maker," for the /**at**/ chunk (page 42). Ask students to cut out the letters at the bottom of the section. Point out the box containing the chunk and ask them to put /**f**/ on the line in the box. Give them time to blend the beginning sound with the chunk before asking someone to read the word they made. Do several examples together before inviting students to work independently.

Explain that only some of the beginning sounds will combine with the chunk to make a real word. Other combinations will make a nonsense word. Model testing for a real word like this, "If I put /**f**/ with /**at**/ I can

make the word *fat*. I know that word because my cat is fat. However, /**d**/ and /**at**/ make /**dat**/. I've never heard of that word." Give students several minutes to work with their word maker independently before asking them to share the words they have made. Discuss which beginning sounds made real words and which did not.

Finally, point out that there wasn't room on the word maker to include all the words for the /**at**/ chunk. For example, the word flat has the /**at**/ chunk. Ask the group, "How would I spell flat? Is the beginning sound for flat on the word builder? What other /**at**/ words do you know? How would you spell them?" (Suggestion: Give each child a self-sealing plastic bag with his or her name and the chunk on it. Have students enclose the pieces in the bags for later practice.)

Now pass out the "Chunk, Write, Draw" work sheet on page 36. Students will choose four real words containing /**at**/ and write each on a line in one of the boxes on their work sheet. They can use their Word Maker or other /**at**/ words they are able to spell accurately. Remind them that they need to choose words they can illustrate, such as bat. Find the first box on the work sheet. Model writing the word *bat* on the line and drawing a bat in the box below the word. Then ask, "Could we use the word *that*? Why not?"

Daily Plans for the Week (cont.)

▼◁▲▽◁▲▽◁▲▽◁▲▽◁▲▽◁▲▽◁▲▽◁▲▽▷▲▽▷▲▽▷▲▽▷▲▽

Wednesday (cont.)

Finally, remind students to circle the box with their best /**at**/ word, neatest handwriting, and clearest drawing. Tell them you will be selecting work that is well done to put into the dictionary. Cut out word/picture boxes from the work of a variety of children and glue them to the right-hand page for that chunk in the Class Chunking Dictionary. Store this dictionary in a prominent place, such as the writing center, to allow children to use it to practice chunking and as a reference tool.

Assessment

This activity also works well as an assessment tool. You will probably notice some students having difficulty blending the beginning sound with the chunk. These children would benefit from small group reteaching with the chunking computers, dry wipes, and/or manipulative letters. Others may be unable to remember the sound for each chunk. These children may need their own set of chunk flash cards.

Making Chunk Flash Cards

Ask volunteers to complete the following tasks:

1. Gather small index cards, metal rings, two copies per student of the Student Word Chunks (pages 56–60), scissors, hole punch, and glue sticks.

2. Using a copy of the Student Word Chunks, cut out the chunks that the students have studied, minus the picture and beginning letters. Glue these chunks to one side of an index card.

3. Using the second copy of pages 56–60, cut out the boxes along the dotted lines. Glue these to the other side of the index card, matching the chunks.

4. Punch a hole in the upper left corner of the side with just the chunk.

5. Put the cards on a ring for each child who needs extra practice.

These cards can be used at school or home for extra practice. Start by making a ring of five of the chunks that have been taught. Children can practice on their own by saying the chunk and turning the card to self-check.

Choose a down time, such as bus dismissal or playground duty, to listen to each child read his/her chunk cards to you. Each time the student gives the correct sound for a chunk, put a star on the card. When the child has five stars, the card can come off the ring and another chunk can be added. This is also a good activity for home practice.

Daily Plans for the Week (cont.)

Thursday

Using the Student Word Chunks

Ask your class to locate their Student Word Chunks in their chunking folder. Review the way in which words are arranged. Use leading questions like, "Where would we find the /at/ chunk?" to allow them to discover the alphabetical arrangement by vowel. When they locate the /at/ chunk, model highlighting the chunk with a yellow crayon and invite students to do the same. Gradually, allow them to become more independent at finding and highlighting the chunk of the week.

Select a writing activity that involves the whole class, such as morning news or a class letter. When a word containing a known chunk is needed, ask students for the beginning sound. Then ask them to use their student word chunks to find and spell the chunk they hear at the end of the word. Some students will prefer to use the large class chunk wall and this is fine. Other students will do better focusing on a small copy close to them. Continue to use the chunk wall in this way throughout the day to integrate this new knowledge into ongoing class activities.

Using the Class Chunking Dictionary

The use of this reference tool can be modeled in much the same way as the Student Word Chunks. Help students discover the alphabetical-by-vowel arrangement of the chunks. When a child attempts to write a word containing a known chunk, ask him/her to write the known chunk first. Then he/she can turn to the page for that chunk to see if the word he/she needs is there. When a student discovers a word not included in the chunking dictionary, you will want to add it. Involve the whole class whenever possible. Invite them to discuss and spell the word as you write it on the left side of the dictionary page.

Many students will enjoy reading the Class Chunking Dictionary. For this reason, locate it in a spot where pages can be turned with ease. This activity is great chunking practice.

Introducing the Chunking Contest

The idea of this contest is for the students to figure out what the key word is and then to make as many words as possible by rearranging the letters in as many ways as they can. Begin by selecting a key word from the Chunking Contest Key Words list (page 62). For example, select the key word, *cracker*. Write that word, with the letters in random order, in the dashed squares (one letter per square) at the bottom of the Chunking Contest Work Sheet (page 61). Make copies for every student in the class. The students should then cut out those squares. Have students manipulate the cut squares, using the boxes at the top of their work sheets as a guide for letter placement, to try to figure out the key word.

Daily Plans for the Week (cont.)

▼◀▲▼◀▲▼◀▲▼◀▲▼◀▲▼◀▲▼◀▲▼◀▲▼▶▲▼▶▲▼▶▲▼▶▲▼

Thursday (cont.)

Introducing the Chunking Contest

(cont.)

Remind them that they will need to use every letter to determine the correct word. When they figure it out, they should write that word on the line below the boxes.

Next, have students look for new words. Review the Chunking Contest Rules (page 64) regarding letter usage and scoring. Examples of possible words they may find with the letters in cracker include *crack*, *car*, and *race*. You will probably need to do one or two examples with the class.

Have students complete page 61 by writing their new words on the lines. They may enter their papers by submitting them to the teacher, placing them in a contest box or basket, or by some other means of collection. Determine students' scores according to the contest rules. You can display the best entries on a bulletin board or add them to your Chunking Wall. Highlight the words containing the chunk.

Scoring the Contest

Each correctly spelled word that was made with only the letters listed will receive a point. Remind students that there is a key word for each puzzle. The key word uses all the letters given and is worth five points.

The student receiving the most points will be the winner. Remember to ask volunteers to score these contests for you.

Try to give each child a chance to win. To do this, you may need to vary the winning criteria for the day. You might say that five extra points will be given for writing neatly, working quietly, or being kind to others. To discourage guessing, subtract a point for each misspelled word. (These suggestions are also noted on page 64.) Watch to see how your class reacts and vary the awards to make it fun for all. The winner can receive a small prize or certificate of merit for his/her effort. Make the presentation with lots of clapping for good effort.

Friday

Applying New Knowledge in Context

Throughout the week you have been modeling the use of the new chunk in all areas of instruction. During small group reading instruction, you have pulled known chunks into the process. As children have written words containing the chunk of the week, you have referred them to the Chunk Wall to help them spell. Now it is time to see how much they can do on their own.

Daily Plans for the Week (cont.)

▼◄▲▼◄▲▼◄▲▼◄▲▼◄▲▼◄▲▼◄▲▼◄▲▼►▲▼►▲▼►▲▼

Friday (cont.)

Applying New Knowledge in Context *(cont.)*

In preparation for this activity, copy page 70 for each student. Use pages 65–69 to locate the sentence starter for the chunk you are teaching. Write the sentence starter on the chalkboard. (If you haven't used sentence starters with your class, you may wish to model this activity with the class using the sentence starter on page 71.)

Read the sentence starter with the class. Ask students to copy the starter on the first line of their work sheet. Point out to students that the chunk of the week is contained in the sentence starter. Challenge students to think of a way they could finish this sentence to begin their writing. Ask them to discuss their ideas with a buddy. Finally, ask several children to share their ideas with the class. Explain that they will need to complete this sentence and write any additional sentences needed to clearly explain their idea or tell their story. They can use a second sheet of paper if they need more space.

After most children complete this project, remind them of the list at the bottom of the page. Read and explain these revising/editing rules. Remind students to reread and correct their writing to be sure they have followed each rule. (Before you make copies, white-out any of the items on the list you have not taught.)

Remind children they are welcome to use resources in the room to help them, but they may not copy their sentences from somewhere else. Give your students a reasonable length of time to complete this activity on their own. (Please note that beginning writers may only be able to complete a sentence at the beginning of the year. Take your writers from where they are and gently move forward.)

Assessing Results

To allow you to measure growth, save a writing sample from September, January, and the end of the year for each student. Read each writing sample and highlight any chunks taught to date that were used to correctly spell a word. Check any revising/editing rules used consistently. Make a copy of the Assessment Record sheet on page 15 and record the number of checked editing/revising items and the number of highlighted chunks for each student.

Compare data from one sample to the next to see how well your instruction is working. Note those students who are still using few chunks to spell or who have editing/revising problems. If most students are struggling with a particular area, this can be your next teaching point for the entire group. Those concepts that are not grasped by just a small number of students should be addressed in a small-group situation.

You can also use this information to communicate with parents and colleagues. It will enable professionals to work together to address the specific needs of each child.

Assessment Record

Name	Number of Chunks Used Correctly			Correct Punctuation*			Writing Makes Sense: (Y) or (N)	Notes
	Sept.	Jan.	June	Capitals	End Punctuation	Lines and Finger Spaces		

* A = all the time   S = some of the time   R = rarely

The Chunking Computer

Name _____

Fold back.

cut

cut

fold

cut

cut

Fold back and tape.

Computer Word Strips

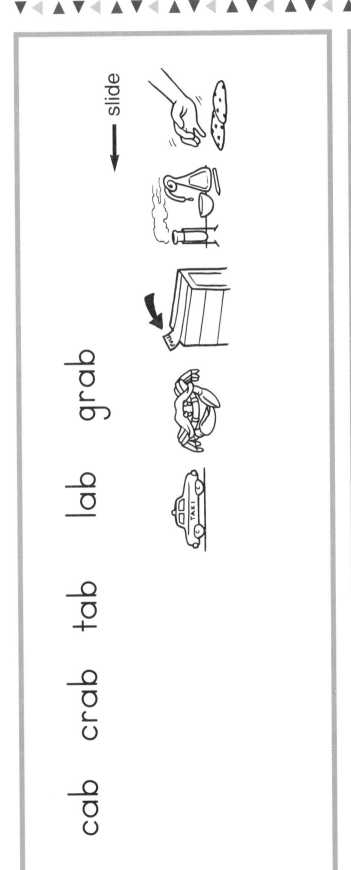

cab crab tab lab grab

slide →

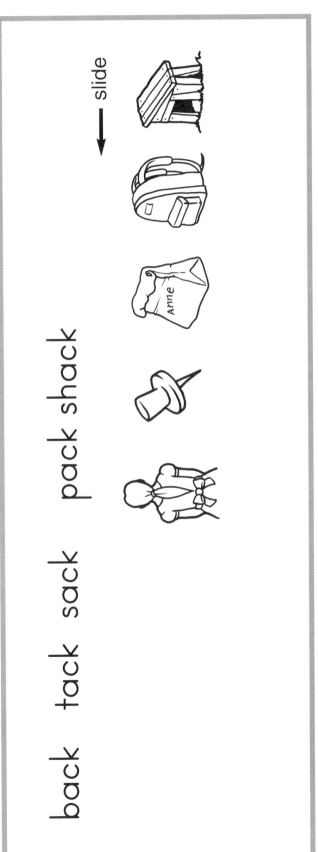

back tack sack pack shack

slide →

Computer Word Strips (cont.)

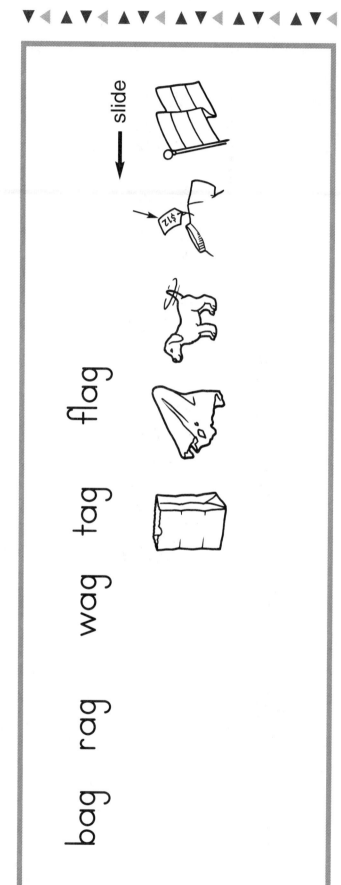

18

Computer Word Strips (cont.)

rain chain grain train brain

slide

cake lake rake wake snake

slide

Computer Word Strips (cont.)

slide

ham jam ram yam clam

slide

can fan man pan van

20

Computer Word Strips (cont.)

bank tank sank drank Hank

cap map nap lap clap

Computer Word Strips (cont.)

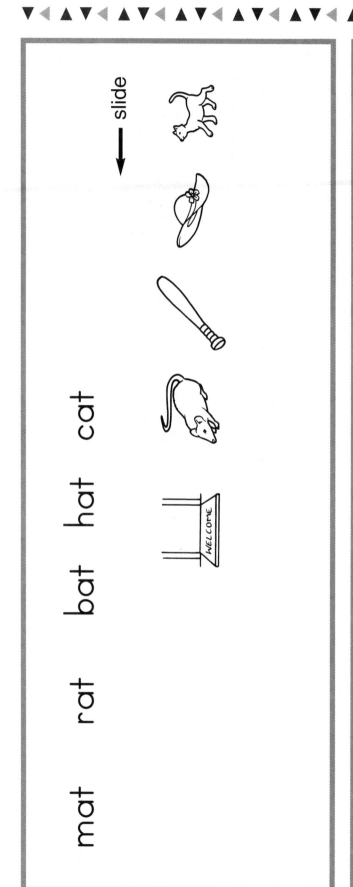

mat   rat   bat   hat   cat   → slide

hay   jay   clay   spray   tray   → slide

Computer Word Strips (cont.)

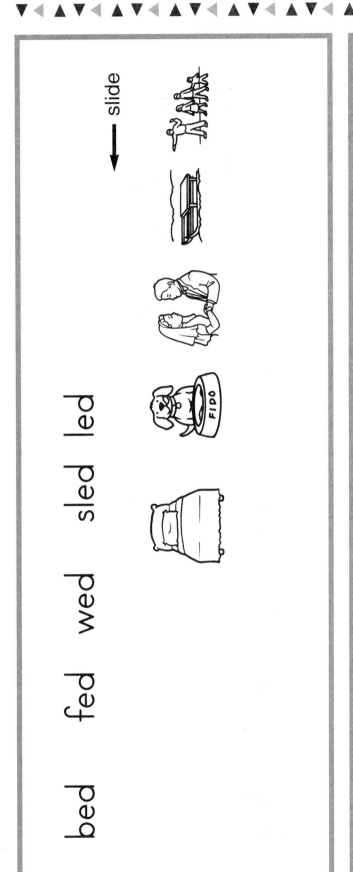

bed   fed   wed   sled   led

seed   weed   feed   reed   speed

Computer Word Strips (cont.)

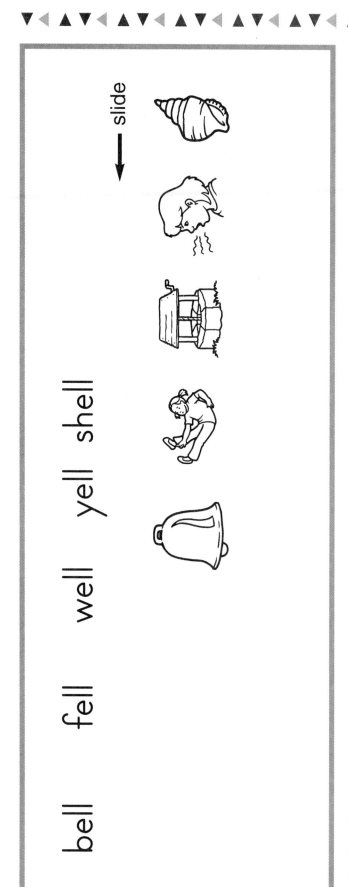

bell   fell   well   yell   shell

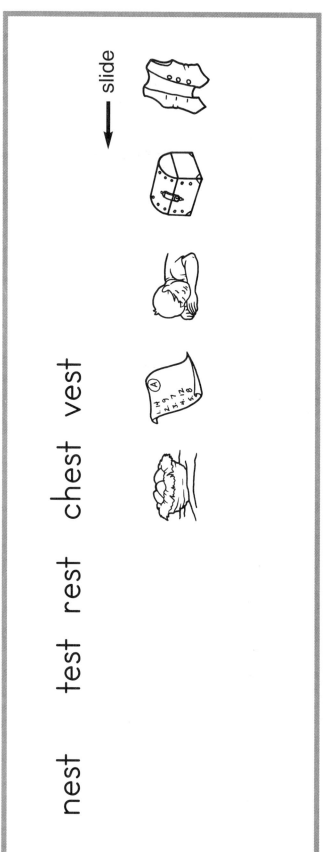

nest   test   rest   chest   vest

Computer Word Strips (cont.)

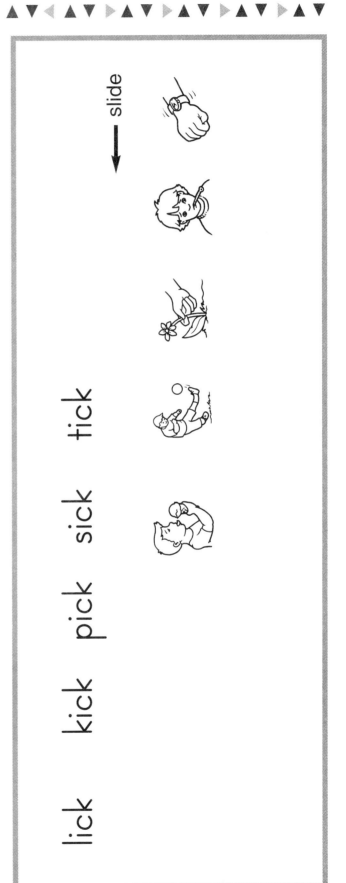

blew   flew   chew   pew   stew

slide

lick   kick   pick   sick   tick

slide

Computer Word Strips (cont.)

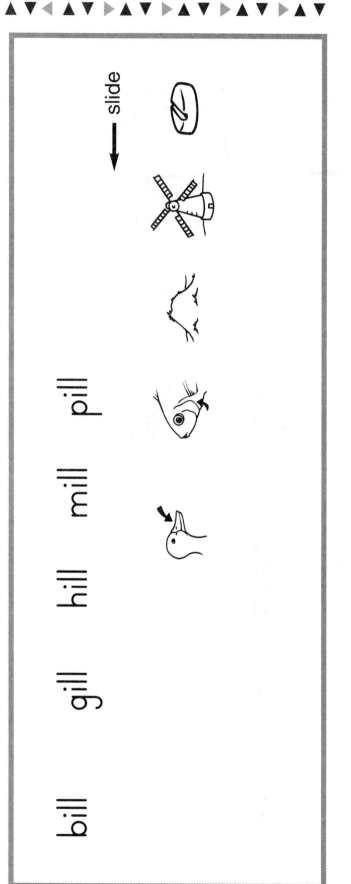

light   tight   right   knight   night

← slide

bill   gill   hill   mill   pill

← slide

26

Computer Word Strips (cont.)

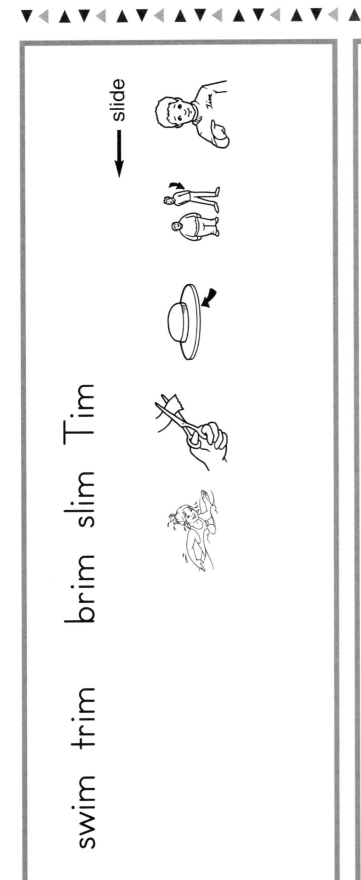

swim trim brim slim Tim

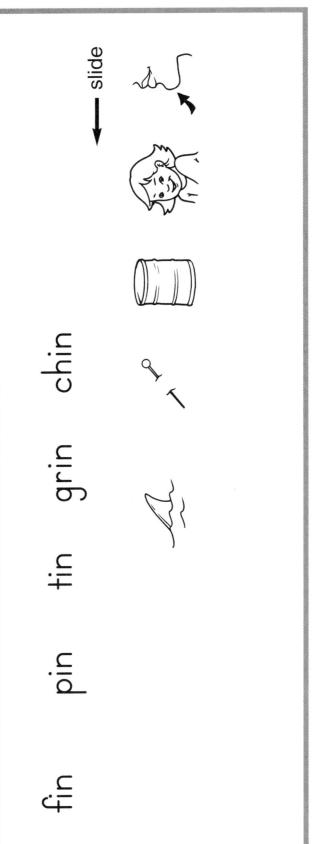

fin pin tin grin chin

Computer Word Strips (cont.)

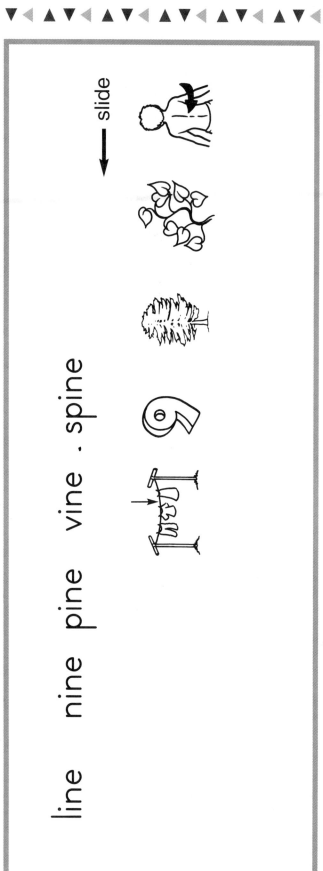

line   nine   pine   vine   . spine

slide

king   ring   wing   sling   swing

slide

28

Computer Word Strips (cont.)

link wink sink mink stink

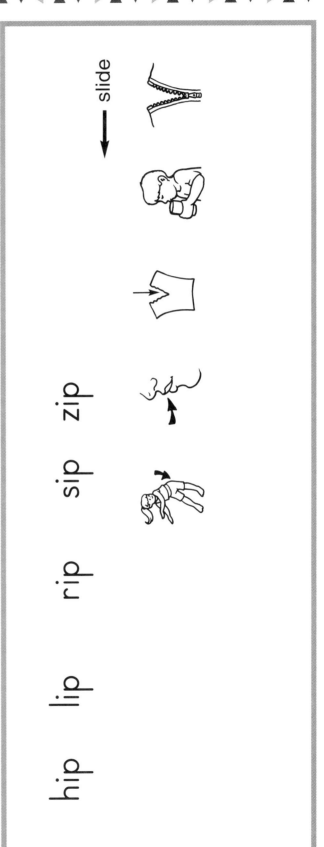

hip lip rip sip zip

Computer Word Strips (cont.)

▼◄▲▼◄▲▼◄▲▼◄▲▼◄▲▼◄▲▼◄▲▼◄▲▼◄▲▼►▲▼►▲▼►▲▼►▲▼

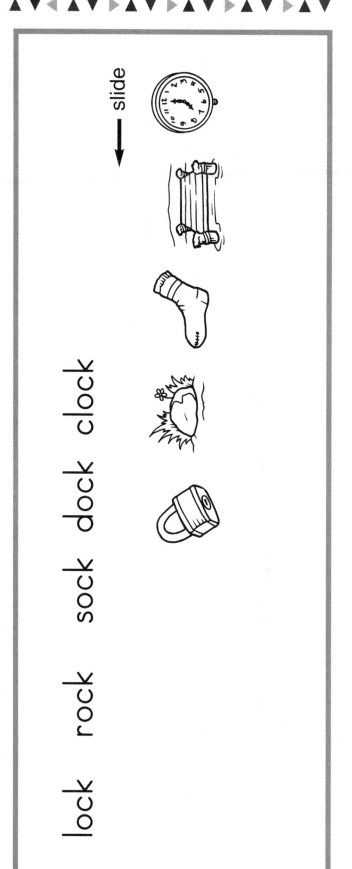

→ slide

cob sob mob knob Bob

lock rock sock dock clock

Computer Word Strips (cont.)

cop hop mop pop top

core tore shore store snore

Computer Word Strips (cont.)

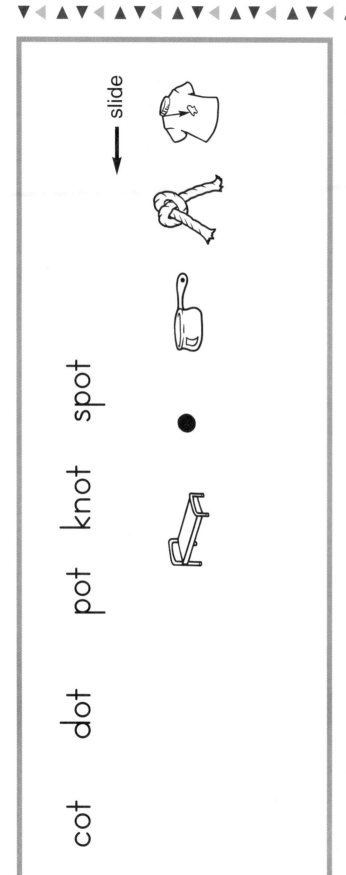

cot   dot   pot   knot   spot

out   scout   shout   trout   sprout

Computer Word Strips <small>(cont.)</small>

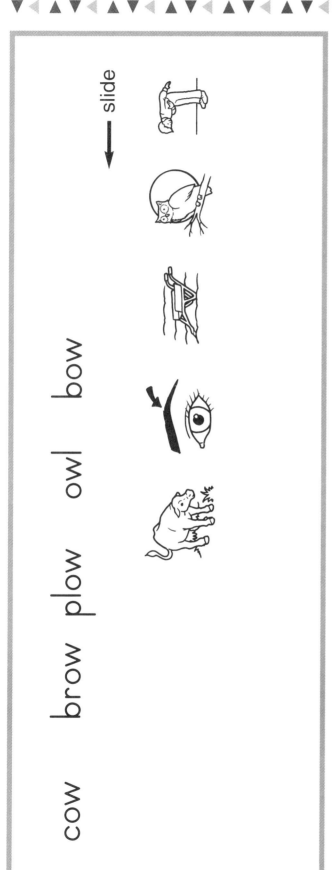

cow   brow   plow   owl   bow

→ slide

duck   suck   puck   buck   truck

→ slide

Computer Word Strips (cont.)

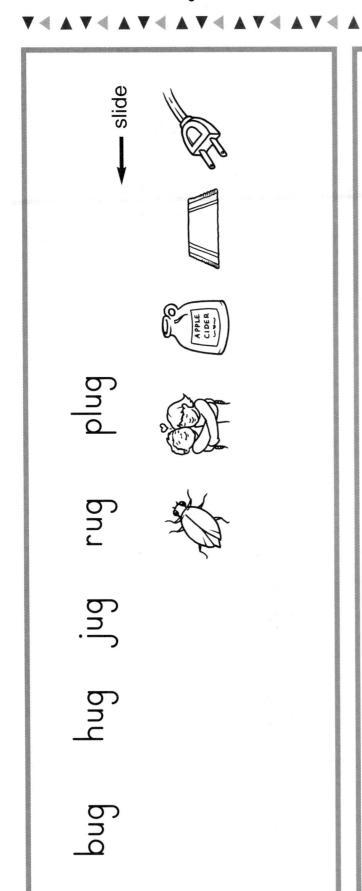

bug   hug   jug   rug   plug

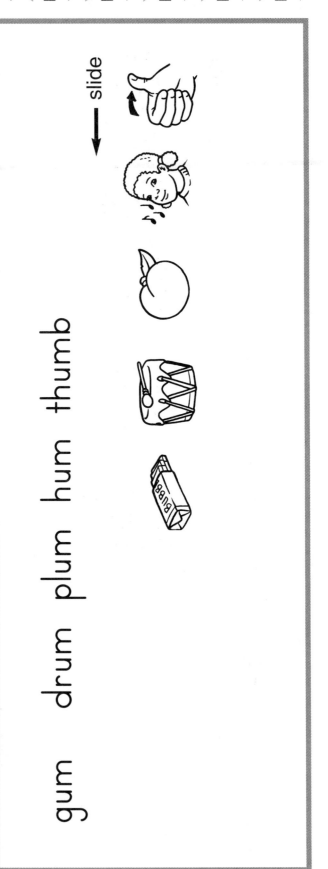

gum   drum   plum   hum   thumb

34

Computer Word Strips (cont.)

bunk   sunk   dunk   skunk   trunk

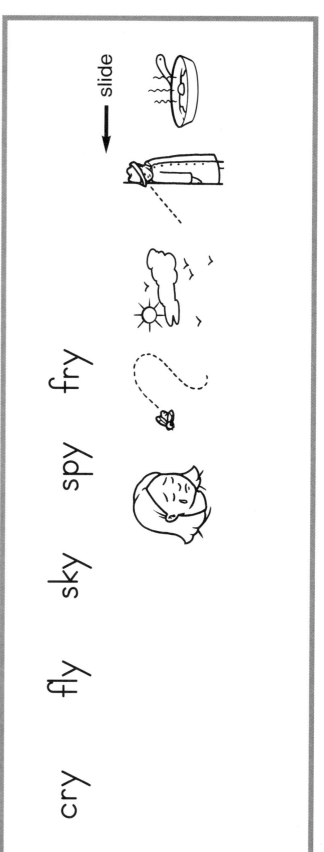

cry   fly   sky   spy   fry

Chunk, Write, Draw

▼◄▲▼◄▲▼◄▲▼◄▲▼◄▲▼◄▲▼◄▲▼◄▲▼►▲▼►▲▼►▲▼►▲▼

Name _____

Directions

- Use the chunk of the week to make four words you can draw.
- Write the words on the lines in the boxes below.
- Draw a picture in each box to illustrate the word.
- Circle the box with your best picture-word, clearest drawing, and neatest handwriting. Your teacher may use it in the class picture dictionary!

Word Makers

Name _____ Word Maker #1

Directions

- Cut out the letter boxes at the bottom of this section.
- Place one letter box on the line next to the chunk.
- Say the sound for the letter and then say the chunk. Did you hear a word you know?
- Which letter sound does not combine with the chunk to make a real word?

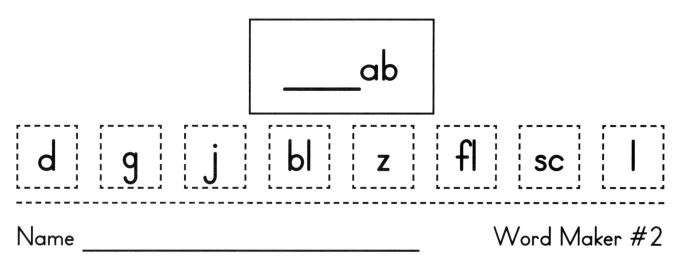

Name _____ Word Maker #2

Directions

- Cut out the letter boxes at the bottom of this section.
- Place one letter box on the line next to the chunk.
- Say the sound for the letter and then say the chunk. Did you hear a word you know?
- Which letter sound does not combine with the chunk to make a real word?

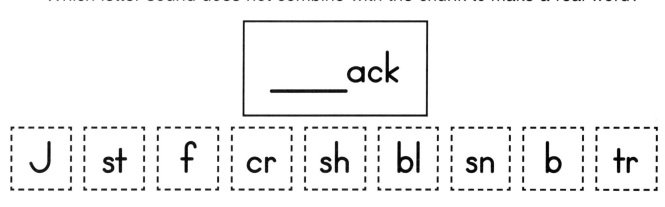

Word Makers (cont.)

Directions

- Cut out the letter boxes at the bottom of this section.
- Place one letter box on the line next to the chunk.
- Say the sound for the letter and then say the chunk. Did you hear a word you know?
- Which letter sound does not combine with the chunk to make a real word?

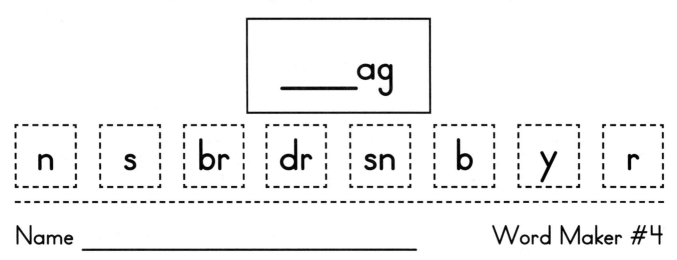

Directions

- Cut out the letter boxes at the bottom of this section.
- Place one letter box on the line next to the chunk.
- Say the sound for the letter and then say the chunk. Did you hear a word you know?
- Which letter sound does not combine with the chunk to make a real word?

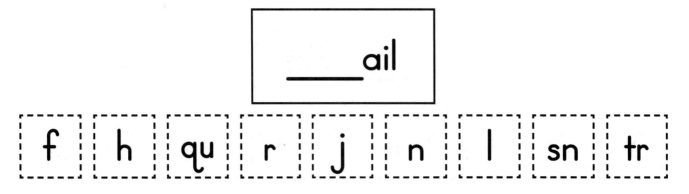

Word Makers (cont.)

Directions

- Cut out the letter boxes at the bottom of this section.
- Place one letter box on the line next to the chunk.
- Say the sound for the letter and then say the chunk. Did you hear a word you know?
- Which letter sound does not combine with the chunk to make a real word?

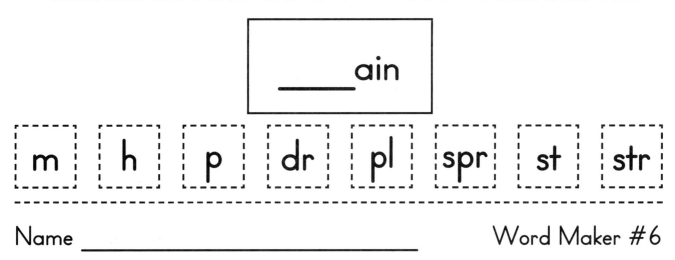

Directions

- Cut out the letter boxes at the bottom of this section.
- Place one letter box on the line next to the chunk.
- Say the sound for the letter and then say the chunk. Did you hear a word you know?
- Which letter sound does not combine with the chunk to make a real word?

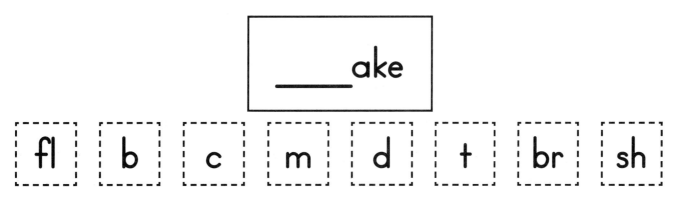

Word Makers (cont.)

▼◄▲▼◄▲▼◄▲▼◄▲▼◄▲▼◄▲▼◄▲▼◄▲▼►▲▼►▲▼►▲▼►▲▼

Name _____   Word Maker #7

Directions

- Cut out the letter boxes at the bottom of this section.
- Place one letter box on the line next to the chunk.
- Say the sound for the letter and then say the chunk. Did you hear a word you know?
- Which letter sound does not combine with the chunk to make a real word?

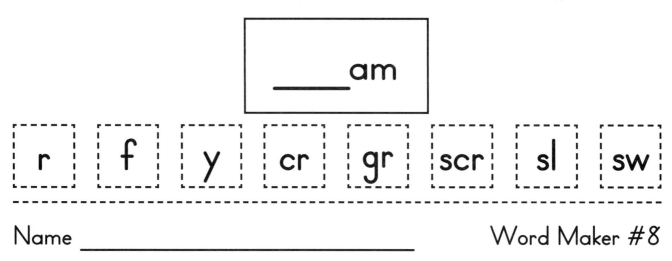

| r | f | y | cr | gr | scr | sl | sw |

Name _____   Word Maker #8

Directions

- Cut out the letter boxes at the bottom of this section.
- Place one letter box on the line next to the chunk.
- Say the sound for the letter and then say the chunk. Did you hear a word you know?
- Which letter sound does not combine with the chunk to make a real word?

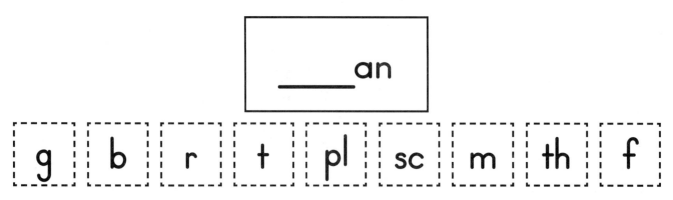

| g | b | r | t | pl | sc | m | th | f |

Word Makers (cont.)

Name _____ Word Maker #9

Directions

- Cut out the letter boxes at the bottom of this section.
- Place one letter box on the line next to the chunk.
- Say the sound for the letter and then say the chunk. Did you hear a word you know?
- Which letter sound does not combine with the chunk to make a real word?

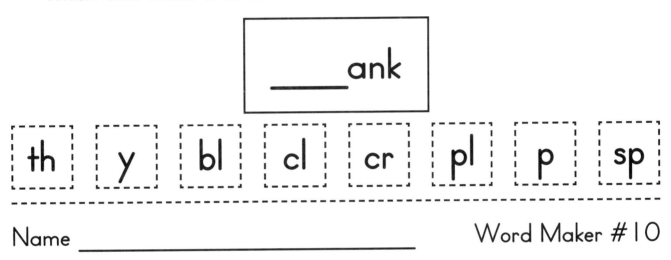

Name _____ Word Maker #10

Directions

- Cut out the letter boxes at the bottom of this section.
- Place one letter box on the line next to the chunk.
- Say the sound for the letter and then say the chunk. Did you hear a word you know?
- Which letter sound does not combine with the chunk to make a real word?

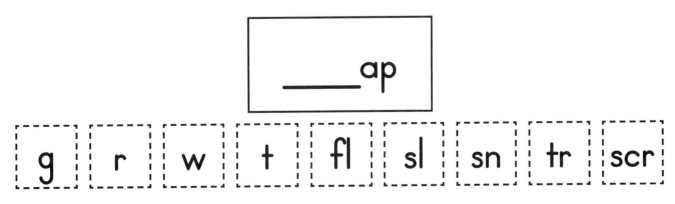

© Teacher Created Materials, Inc. 41 #3287 Word Chunks

Word Makers (cont.)

Name _____ Word Maker #11

Directions

- Cut out the letter boxes at the bottom of this section.
- Place one letter box on the line next to the chunk.
- Say the sound for the letter and then say the chunk. Did you hear a word you know?
- Which letter sound does not combine with the chunk to make a real word?

____at

f	p	s	b	fl	th	d	sc

Name _____ Word Maker #12

Directions

- Cut out the letter boxes at the bottom of this section.
- Place one letter box on the line next to the chunk.
- Say the sound for the letter and then say the chunk. Did you hear a word you know?
- Which letter sound does not combine with the chunk to make a real word?

____ay

z	m	l	d	s	b	w	cl	gr

Word Makers (cont.)

Name _____

Directions

- Cut out the letter boxes at the bottom of this section.
- Place one letter box on the line next to the chunk.
- Say the sound for the letter and then say the chunk. Did you hear a word you know?
- Which letter sound does not combine with the chunk to make a real word?

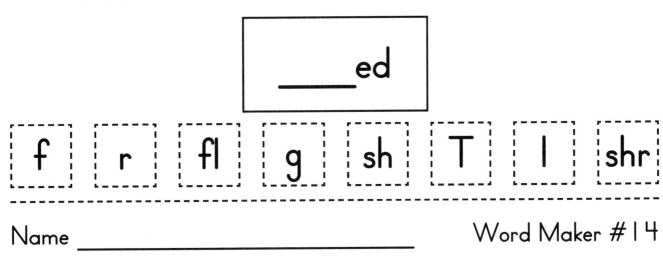

Name _____

Directions

- Cut out the letter boxes at the bottom of this section.
- Place one letter box on the line next to the chunk.
- Say the sound for the letter and then say the chunk. Did you hear a word you know?
- Which letter sound does not combine with the chunk to make a real word?

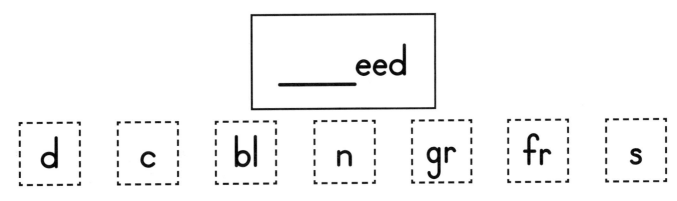

Word Makers (cont.)

▽◁▲▽◁▲▽◁▲▽◁▲▽◁▲▽◁▲▽◁▲▽◁▲▽▷▲▽▷▲▽▷▲▽▷▲▽

Name _____

Directions

- Cut out the letter boxes at the bottom of this section.
- Place one letter box on the line next to the chunk.
- Say the sound for the letter and then say the chunk. Did you hear a word you know?
- Which letter sound does not combine with the chunk to make a real word?

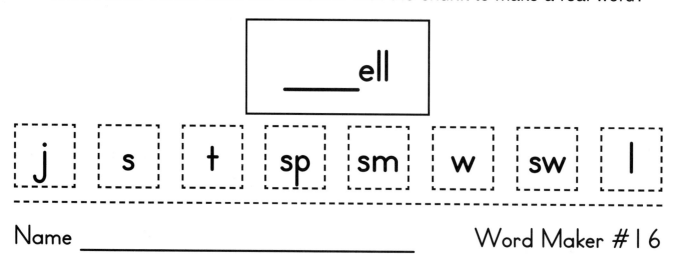

Name _____

Directions

- Cut out the letter boxes at the bottom of this section.
- Place one letter box on the line next to the chunk.
- Say the sound for the letter and then say the chunk. Did you hear a word you know?
- Which letter sound does not combine with the chunk to make a real word?

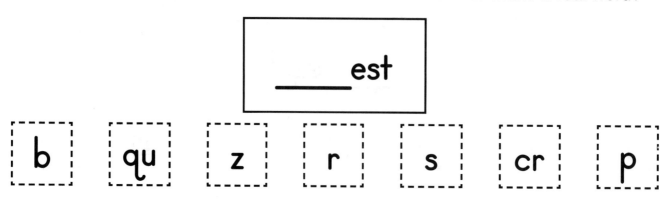

Word Makers (cont.)

Directions

- Cut out the letter boxes at the bottom of this section.
- Place one letter box on the line next to the chunk.
- Say the sound for the letter and then say the chunk. Did you hear a word you know?
- Which letter sound does not combine with the chunk to make a real word?

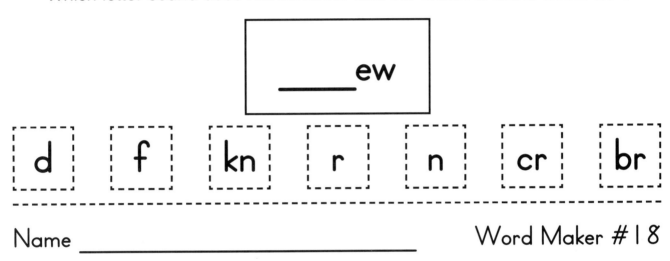

_____ew

| d | f | kn | r | n | cr | br |

Directions

- Cut out the letter boxes at the bottom of this section.
- Place one letter box on the line next to the chunk.
- Say the sound for the letter and then say the chunk. Did you hear a word you know?
- Which letter sound does not combine with the chunk to make a real word?

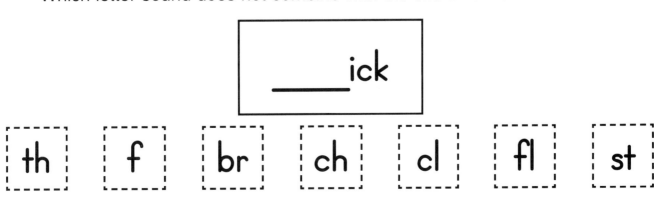

_____ick

| th | f | br | ch | cl | fl | st |

Word Makers (cont.)

Directions

- Cut out the letter boxes at the bottom of this section.
- Place one letter box on the line next to the chunk.
- Say the sound for the letter and then say the chunk. Did you hear a word you know?
- Which letter sound does not combine with the chunk to make a real word?

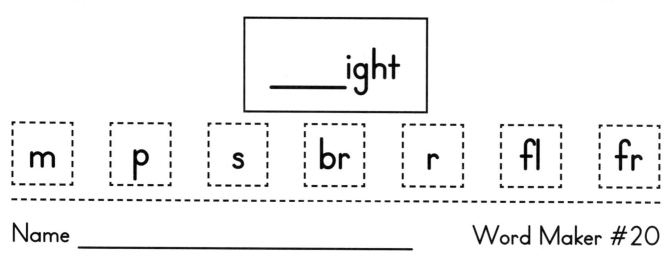

Directions

- Cut out the letter boxes at the bottom of this section.
- Place one letter box on the line next to the chunk.
- Say the sound for the letter and then say the chunk. Did you hear a word you know?
- Which letter sound does not combine with the chunk to make a real word?

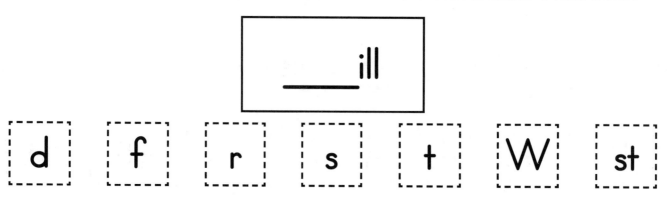

Word Makers (cont.)

Name _____

Directions

- Cut out the letter boxes at the bottom of this section.
- Place one letter box on the line next to the chunk.
- Say the sound for the letter and then say the chunk. Did you hear a word you know?
- Which letter sound does not combine with the chunk to make a real word?

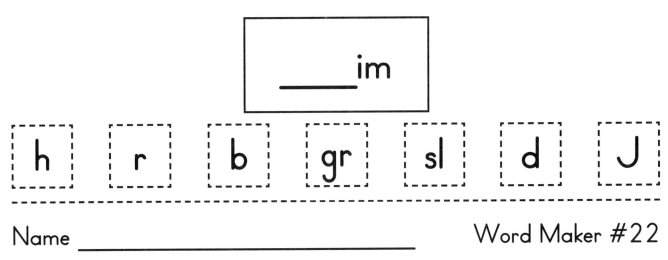

Name _____

Directions

- Cut out the letter boxes at the bottom of this section.
- Place one letter box on the line next to the chunk.
- Say the sound for the letter and then say the chunk. Did you hear a word you know?
- Which letter sound does not combine with the chunk to make a real word?

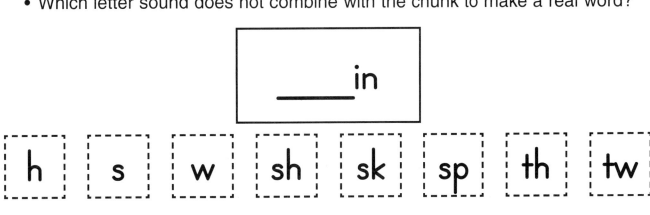

Word Makers (cont.)

Directions

- Cut out the letter boxes at the bottom of this section.
- Place one letter box on the line next to the chunk.
- Say the sound for the letter and then say the chunk. Did you hear a word you know?
- Which letter sound does not combine with the chunk to make a real word?

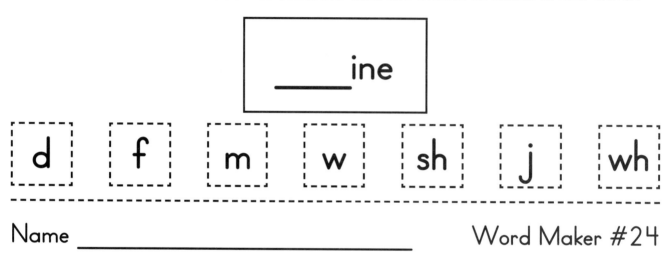

Directions

- Cut out the letter boxes at the bottom of this section.
- Place one letter box on the line next to the chunk.
- Say the sound for the letter and then say the chunk. Did you hear a word you know?
- Which letter sound does not combine with the chunk to make a real word?

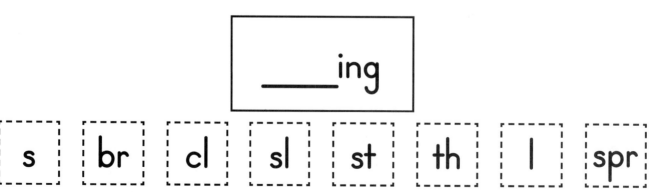

Word Makers (cont.)

Directions

- Cut out the letter boxes at the bottom of this section.
- Place one letter box on the line next to the chunk.
- Say the sound for the letter and then say the chunk. Did you hear a word you know?
- Which letter sound does not combine with the chunk to make a real word?

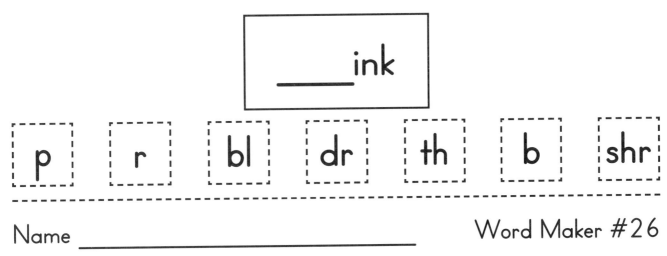

Directions

- Cut out the letter boxes at the bottom of this section.
- Place one letter box on the line next to the chunk.
- Say the sound for the letter and then say the chunk. Did you hear a word you know?
- Which letter sound does not combine with the chunk to make a real word?

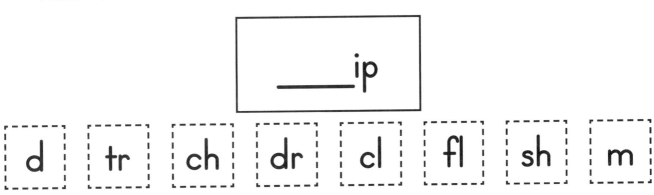

Word Makers (cont.)

Directions

- Cut out the letter boxes at the bottom of this section.
- Place one letter box on the line next to the chunk.
- Say the sound for the letter and then say the chunk. Did you hear a word you know?
- Which letter sound does not combine with the chunk to make a real word?

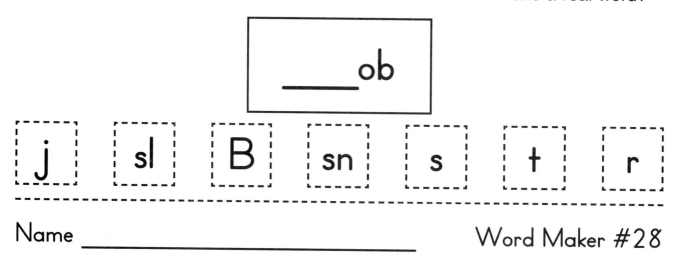

Directions

- Cut out the letter boxes at the bottom of this section.
- Place one letter box on the line next to the chunk.
- Say the sound for the letter and then say the chunk. Did you hear a word you know?
- Which letter sound does not combine with the chunk to make a real word?

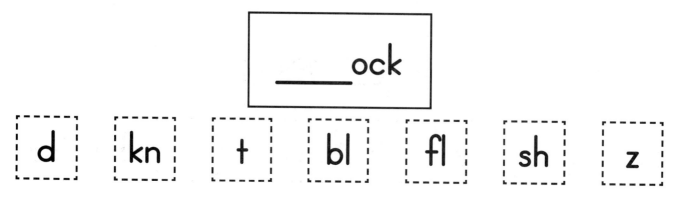

Word Makers (cont.)

Name _____

Directions

- Cut out the letter boxes at the bottom of this section.
- Place one letter box on the line next to the chunk.
- Say the sound for the letter and then say the chunk. Did you hear a word you know?
- Which letter sound does not combine with the chunk to make a real word?

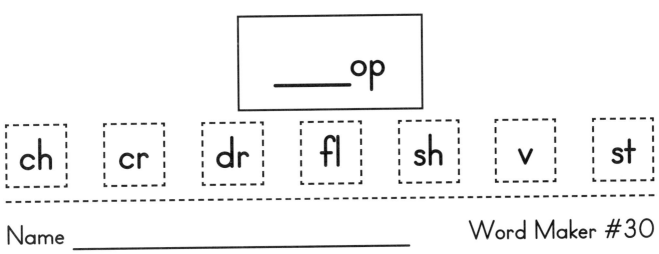

Name _____

Directions

- Cut out the letter boxes at the bottom of this section.
- Place one letter box on the line next to the chunk.
- Say the sound for the letter and then say the chunk. Did you hear a word you know?
- Which letter sound does not combine with the chunk to make a real word?

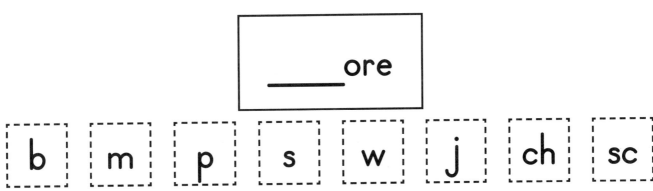

Word Makers (cont.)

Directions

- Cut out the letter boxes at the bottom of this section.
- Place one letter box on the line next to the chunk.
- Say the sound for the letter and then say the chunk. Did you hear a word you know?
- Which letter sound does not combine with the chunk to make a real word?

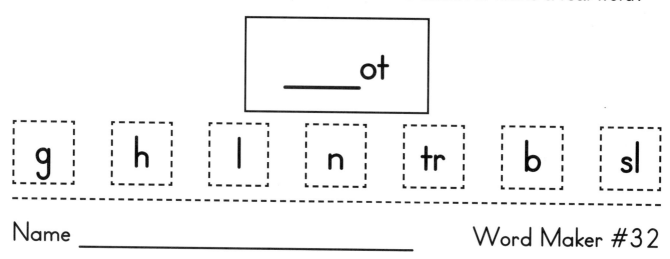

Directions

- Cut out the letter boxes at the bottom of this section.
- Place one letter box on the line next to the chunk.
- Say the sound for the letter and then say the chunk. Did you hear a word you know?
- Which letter sound does not combine with the chunk to make a real word?

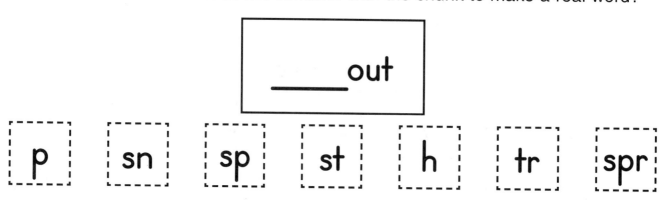

Word Makers (cont.)

Directions

- Cut out the letter boxes at the bottom of this section.
- Place one letter box on the line next to the chunk.
- Say the sound for the letter and then say the chunk. Did you hear a word you know?
- Which letter sound does not combine with the chunk to make a real word?

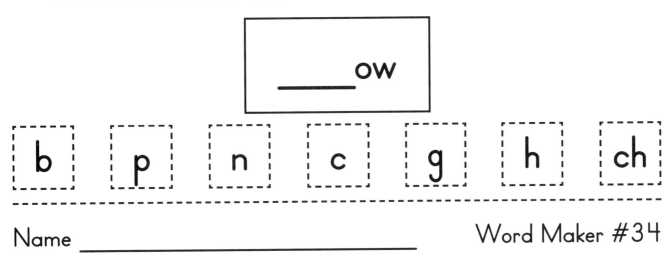

_____ow

| b | p | n | c | g | h | ch |

Directions

- Cut out the letter boxes at the bottom of this section.
- Place one letter box on the line next to the chunk.
- Say the sound for the letter and then say the chunk. Did you hear a word you know?
- Which letter sound does not combine with the chunk to make a real word?

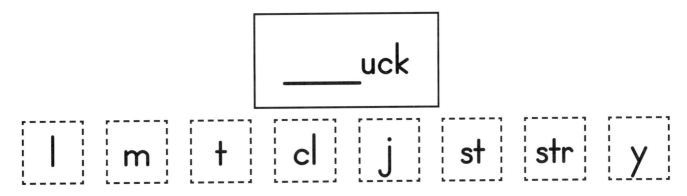

_____uck

| l | m | t | cl | j | st | str | y |

Word Makers (cont.)

Name ________________________ Word Maker #35

Directions

- Cut out the letter boxes at the bottom of this section.
- Place one letter box on the line next to the chunk.
- Say the sound for the letter and then say the chunk. Did you hear a word you know?
- Which letter sound does not combine with the chunk to make a real word?

_____ug

d	h	t	s	ch	dr	sl	shr

Name ________________________ Word Maker #36

Directions

- Cut out the letter boxes at the bottom of this section.
- Place one letter box on the line next to the chunk.
- Say the sound for the letter and then say the chunk. Did you hear a word you know?
- Which letter sound does not combine with the chunk to make a real word?

_____um

b	h	s	l	sc	sl	dr

Word Makers (cont.)

Directions

- Cut out the letter boxes at the bottom of this section.
- Place one letter box on the line next to the chunk.
- Say the sound for the letter and then say the chunk. Did you hear a word you know?
- Which letter sound does not combine with the chunk to make a real word?

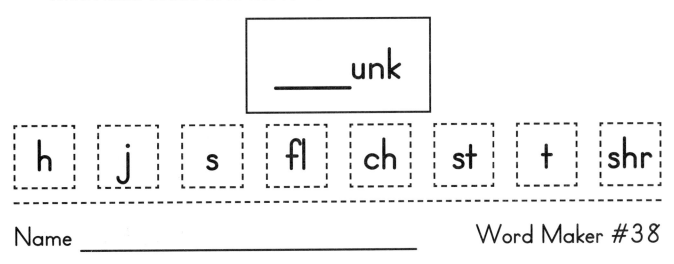

Directions

- Cut out the letter boxes at the bottom of this section.
- Place one letter box on the line next to the chunk.
- Say the sound for the letter and then say the chunk. Did you hear a word you know?
- Which letter sound does not combine with the chunk to make a real word?

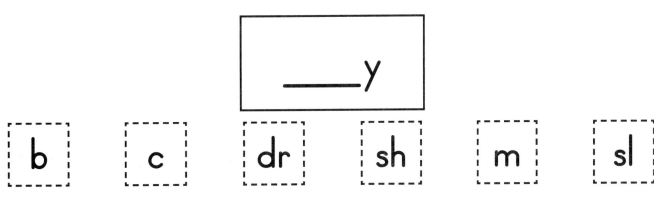

Student Word Chunks

Aa

 cab

 tack

 bag

 pail

 rain

 cake

 jam

 can

 bank

 cap

 cat

 hay

56

Student Word Chunks (cont.)

Name _____

Ee

 **b**ed

 seed

 **b**ell

 vest

 **bl**ew

Student Word Chunks (cont.)

Name _____

Ii

 br**ick**

 h**ill**

 p**in**

 sw**ing**

 z**ip**

 l**ight**

 sw**im**

 n**ine**

 s**ink**

Student Word Chunks (cont.)

Name _____

Oo

 cob

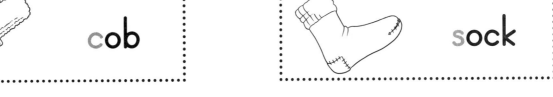 sock

 mop

 core

 pot

 scout

 cow

Student Word Chunks (cont.)

Name _____

Uu

duck

bug

gum

skunk

Yy

fly

Chunking Contest Work Sheet

Name _____

Directions

- Cut out the letter boxes at the bottom of the page. Arrange the letter boxes in the blank boxes below to make a real word. Write your new word on the line below.

⬜ ⬜ ⬜ ⬜ ⬜ ⬜ ⬜ ⬜

_____

- Use the blank box below to arrange the letter boxes to make more new words. How many other words did you make? Write your new words on the lines at the bottom of the page. If you need more space, use the back of this paper. Enter these words in the contest.

_____

_____

_____

_____

Chunking Contest

▼◄▲▼◄▲▼◄▲▼◄▲▼◄▲▼◄▲▼◄▲▼◄▲▼►▲▼►▲▼►▲▼►▲▼

Key Words

Teacher Directions: Locate the key word next to your current chunk. Write the letters for the key word, in mixed-up order in the dotted-line boxes at the bottom of page 61. Make one copy for each student. Follow the directions on pages 12 and 13 for the chunking contest.

Chunk	Key Word	Chunk	Key Word
ab	grabbed	ill	hilltop
ack	cracker	im	swimsuit
ag	baggy	in	twins
ail	sailboat	ine	valentine
ain	sprain	ing	spring
ake	flakes	ink	stinks
am	hamster	ip	flippers
an	sandwich	ob	slobber
ank	tankers	ock	clocks
ap	apples	op	toppings
at	rattle	ore	snored
ay	Saturday	ot	bottle
ed	sledding	out	sprout
eed	speed	ow	brownie
ell	yellow	uck	struck
est	western	ug	shrugged
ew	chewing	um	gumdrop
ick	pickles	unk	shrunk
ight	flashlight	y	myself

How Many Words Can You Make?

JOIN OUR WORD CHUNK CONTEST!

Who? _____

When? _____

How? _____

Chunking Contest Rules

General Rules

1. Words may be listed on the contest paper that do not contain the chunk of the week.

2. All words must be spelled correctly to earn a point.

3. Students may need only one letter to make their word or they may need as many as all of the letters.

4. Students can only use a letter more than once if it is listed more than one time in the boxes.

Scoring the Contest

1. Each correctly spelled word that was made with only the letters listed will receive a point.

2. The key word uses all the letters given and is worth five points.

3. The student receiving the most points will be the winner.

Contest Variations

1. To give each child a chance to win, you may need to vary the winning criteria for the day. You might say that five extra points will be given for writing neatly, working quietly, or being kind to others.

2. To discourage guessing, subtract a point for each misspelled word.

Sentence Starters

Find the chunk your students are learning. Next to it you will find the sentence starter for that chunk. Use this starter for the activity described in the daily plans for Friday.

Chunk	Sentence Starter
ab	I grabbed _____.
ack	My backpack _____.
ag	The bag is _____.
ail	I got the pail _____.
ain	The rain _____.
ake	I make _____.

Sentence Starters (cont.)

▼◄▲▼◄▲▼◄▲▼◄▲▼◄▲▼◄▲▼◄▲▼◄▲▼►▲▼►▲▼►▲▼

Chunk	Sentence Starter
am	I am _____.
an	I ran _____.
ank	Thank you for _____.
ap	I am happy _____.
at	I sat _____.
ay	I play _____.
ed	I fed _____.
eed	I need _____.

Sentence Starters (cont.)

Chunk	Sentence Starter
ell	I fell _____.
est	My best friend _____.
ew	I threw _____.
ick	I got sick _____.
ight	At night I _____.
ill	The silly _____.
im	I help him _____.
in	I can win _____.

Sentence Starters (cont.)

Chunk	Sentence Starter
ine	I get in line for _____.
ing	I sing _____.
ink	I think _____.
ip	My trip _____.
ob	My job is _____.
ock	I lock my _____.
op	I dropped _____.
ore	My sore _____.

68

Sentence Starters (cont.)

Chunk	Sentence Starter
ot	I got a _____.
out	I shout at _____.
ow	How do you _____?
uck	I got stuck _____.
ug	I hug _____.
um	I got gum on _____.
unk	My shoes stunk _____.
y	I am shy _____.

Sentence Starters (cont.)

▼◀ ▲▼◀ ▲▼◀ ▲▼◀ ▲▼◀ ▲▼◀ ▲▼◀ ▲▼◀ ▲▼◀ ▲▼ ▶▲▼ ▶▲▼ ▶▲▼ ▶▲▼

Name _____

Directions

- Finish the sentence on the board. Write more sentences to explain your idea.
- Remember to revise and edit your writing.

_____

- -

_____

_____

- -

_____

_____

- -

_____

_____

- -

_____

How did I do?

- ♦ I wrote on the lines and used finger spaces.
- ♦ I used capital letters only where they were needed.
- ♦ I ended each sentence with a period or a question mark.
- ♦ I used chunks I know to spell words correctly.
- ♦ My writing made sense.
- ♦ _____

Sentence Starters (cont.)

Name _____

Directions

- Finish this sentence. Write more sentences to explain your idea.
- Remember to revise and edit your writing.

I | sat | _____
_____

_____

_____

_____

_____

_____

_____

_____

_____

How did I do?

♦ I wrote on the lines and used finger spaces.

♦ I used capital letters only where they were needed.

♦ I ended each sentence with a period or a question mark.

♦ I used chunks I know to spell words correctly.

♦ My writing made sense.

♦ _____

Chunk Wall

cab

ab

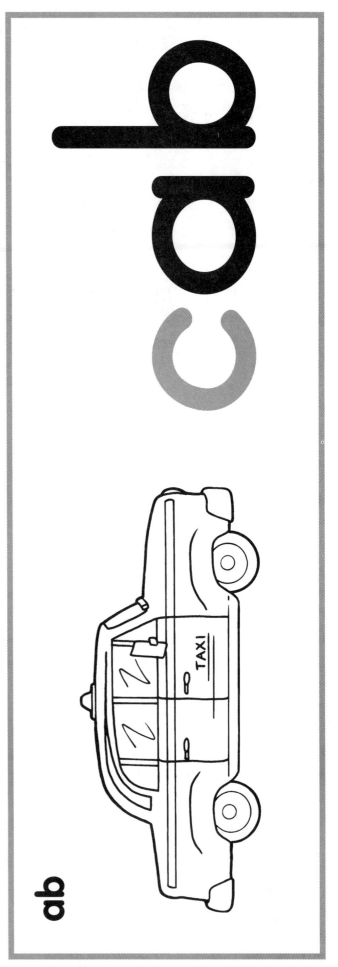

72

tack

ack

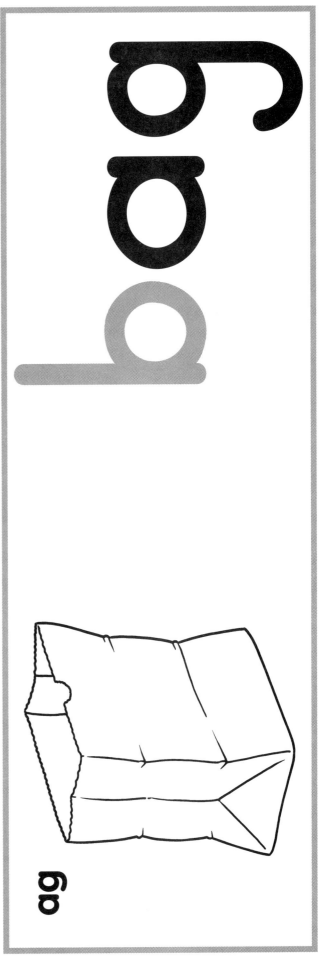

bag

ag

pail

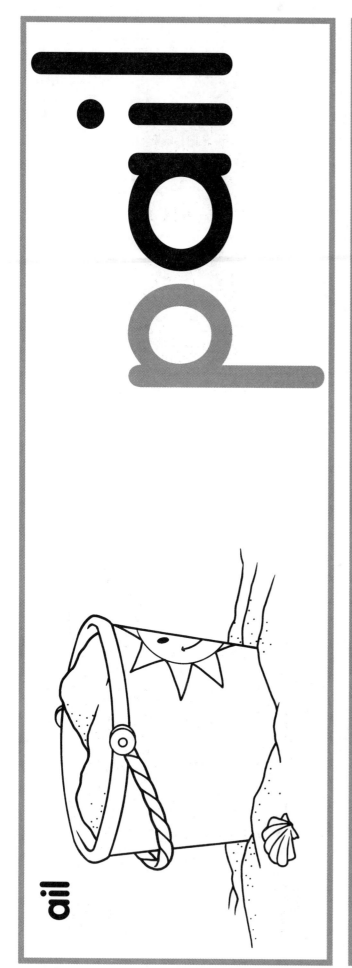

ail

rain

ain

74

cake

ake

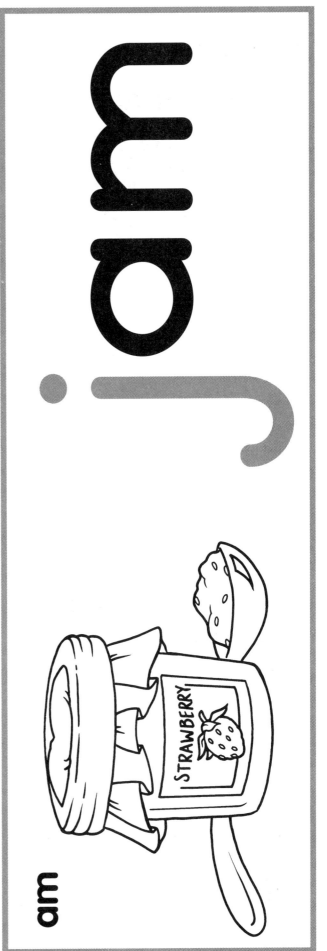

jam

am

can

an

bank

ank

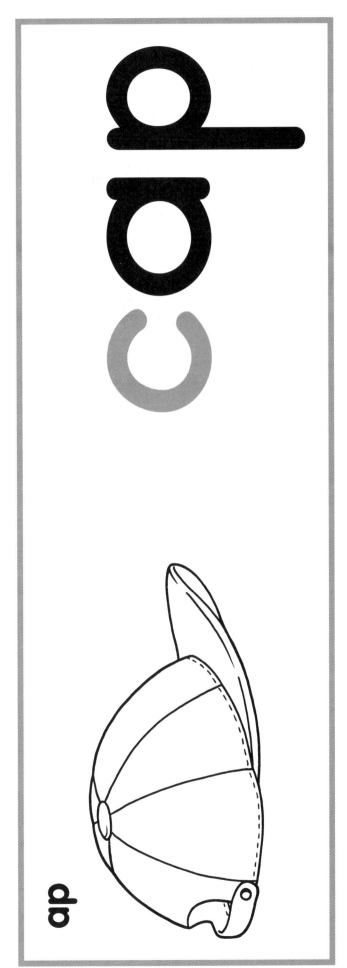

cap

ap

cat

at

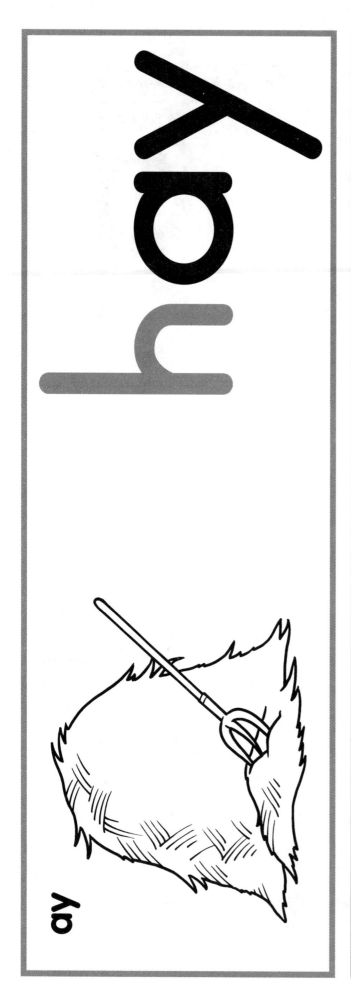

hay

ay

bed

ed

seed

eed

bell

ell

vest

est

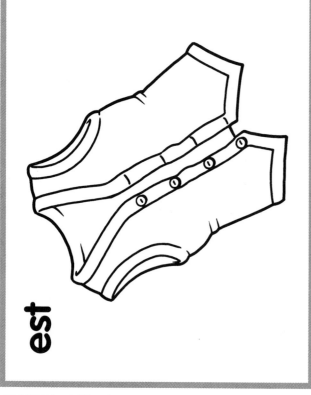

blew

ew

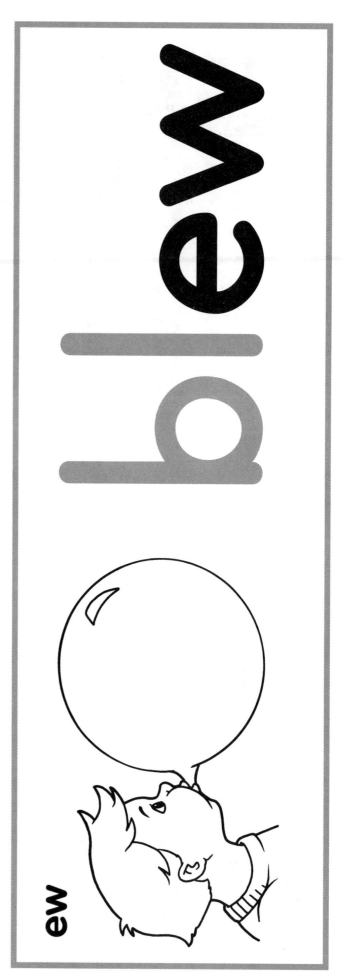

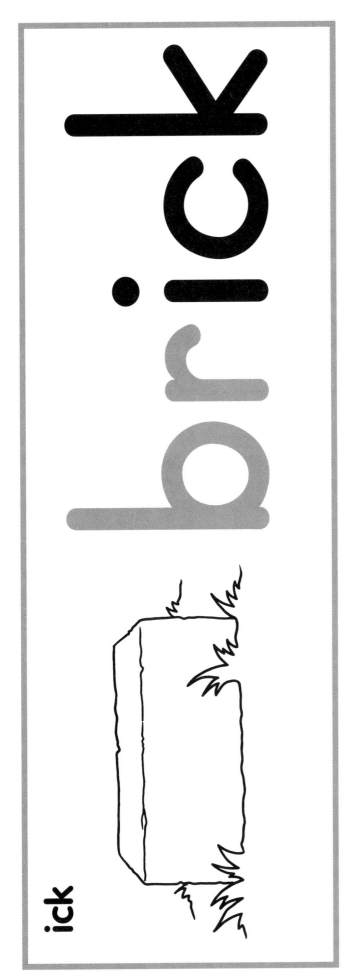

brick

ick

light

ight

hill

ill

swim

im

pin

in

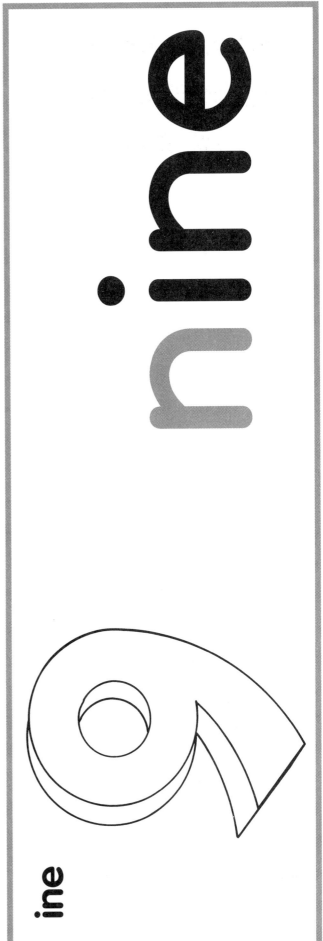

nine

ine

ing

swing

ink

sink

84

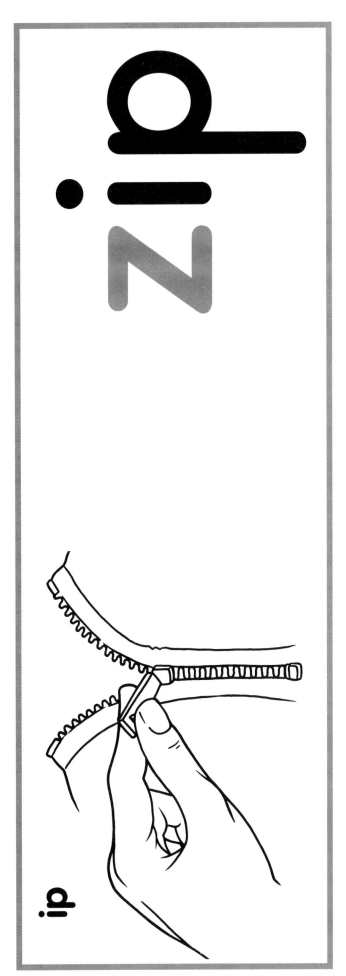

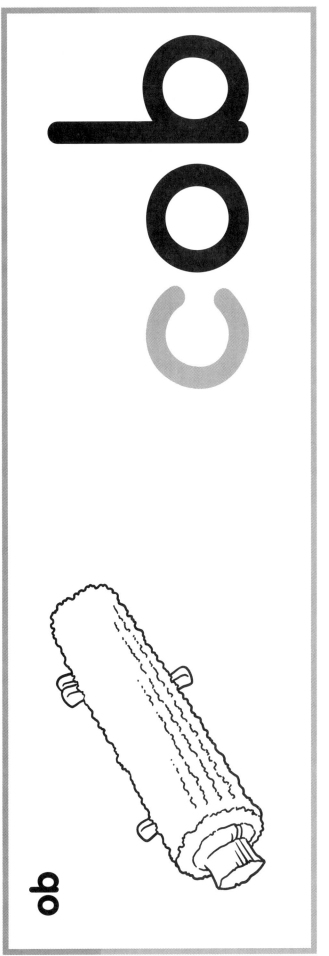

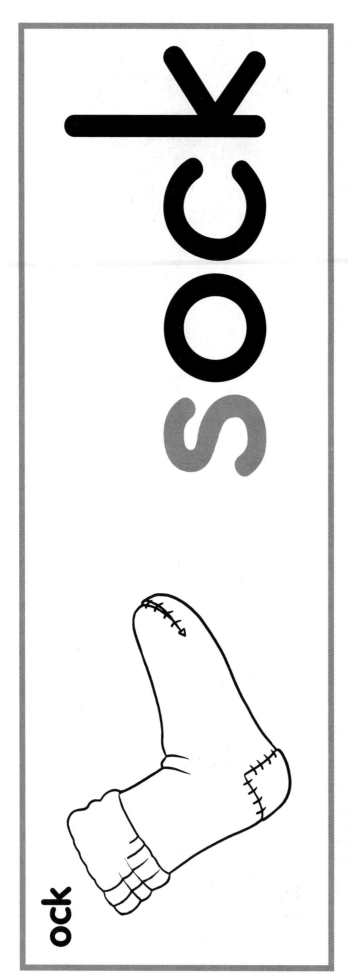

sock

ock

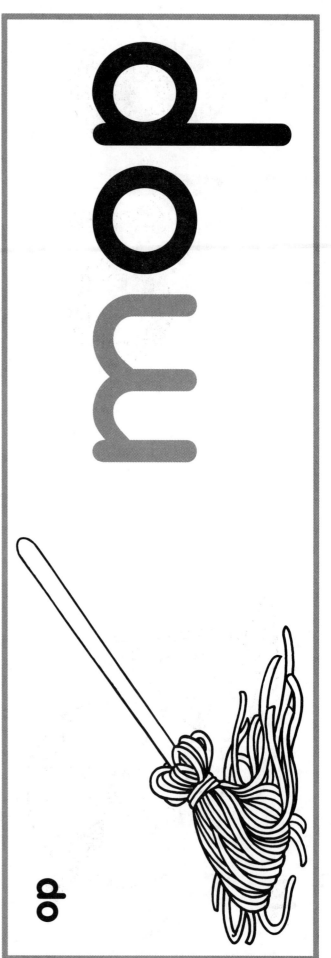

mop

op

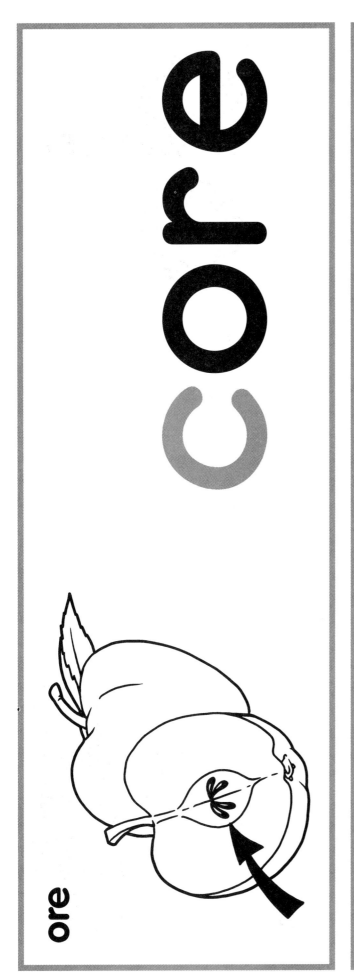

core

ore

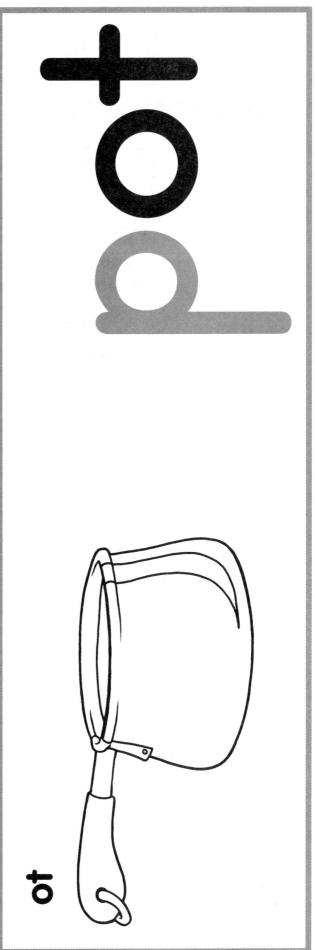

pot

ot

out

scout

ow

cow

88

duck

uck

bug

ug

gum

um

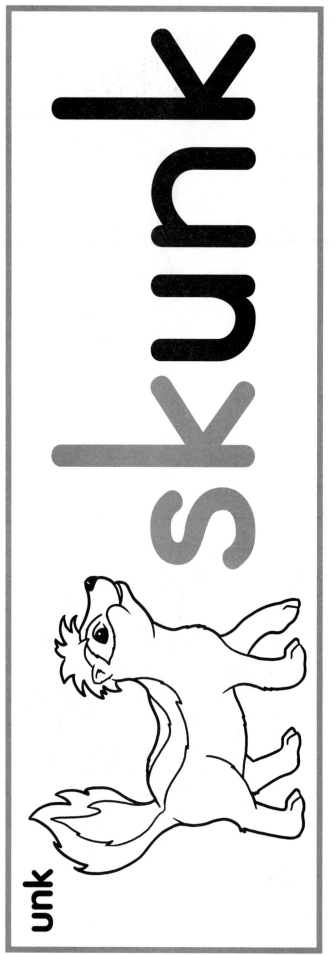

skunk

unk

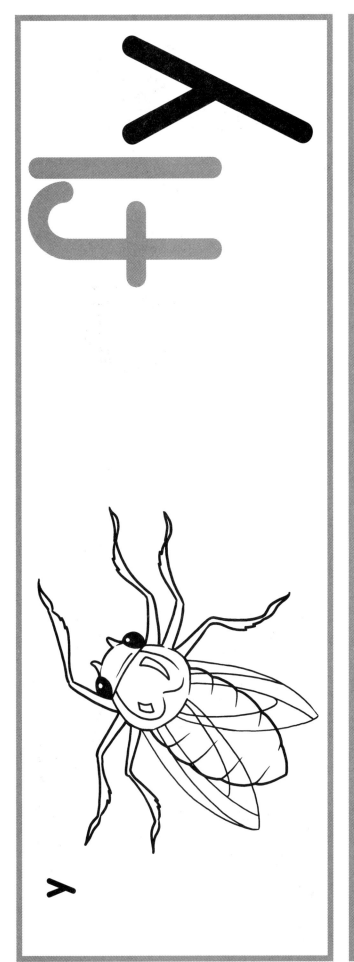

Word Practice Wheel

▼◄▲▼◄▲▼◄▲▼◄▲▼◄▲▼◄▲▼◄▲▼◄▲▼◄▲▼◄▲▼►▲▼►▲▼►▲▼►▲▼

Students can practice reading and recognizing new words with this Word Practice Wheel.

Materials: flash cards (page 93), spinner and arrow (see below), brad, scissors, glue, markers (game pieces, paper clips, paper squares, dried beans, etc.), tagboard or heavy paper

Preparation

Write eight word chunks on the spinner, one on the line in each section. Copy the spinner and pointer (arrow) patterns below onto tagboard or heavy paper. Attach the pointer to the center of the spinner with a brad. (If the pointer is too tight, adjust the bending points of the brad, and/or enlarge the center hole on the pointer.) Write word beginnings on the flash cards on page 93. Reproduce enough flash cards so that each player has a set of word beginnings.

Directions for Playing the Game

Place the spinner and a pile of markers in the center of a small group of students. The first player spins the spinner and says the word chunk on which the pointer stops. (Decide the order of players before starting the game.) He or she then chooses a word beginning from the flash cards that, when added to the chunk, makes a real word. The player says the word. If he or she is correct, the player collects a marker and the game moves on to the next player. If the word is incorrect, the player does not collect a marker and the next player has a turn. The winner is the first child to collect a predetermined number of markers. (Option: You and your students can use the spinner and flash cards to make your own word games.)

Word Practice Wheel _(cont.)

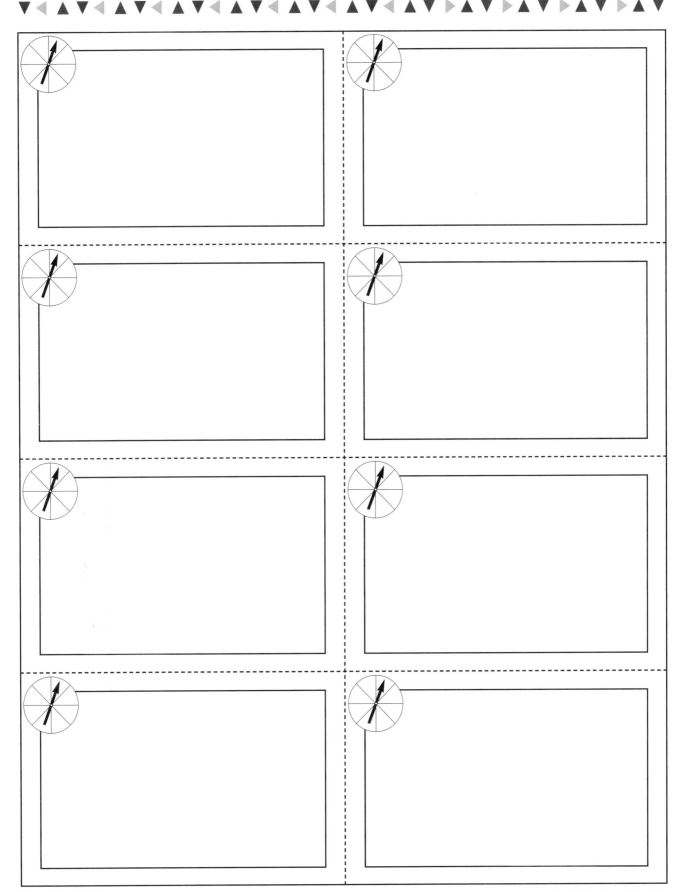

Chunk Word Walk

▼◄▲▼◄▲▼◄▲▼◄▲▼◄▲▼◄▲▼◄▲▼◄▲▼▶▲▼▶▲▼▶▲▼▶▲▼

Students can practice reading and recognizing new words with this activity. Use some of the words from the Computer Word Strips. (For easy reference, see list below.)

Materials: copies of footprints on page 95, markers, laminating materials, music (optional)

Preparation

Reproduce the footprints and write a word on each foot. Cut out the prints and laminate them.

Directions for Playing the Chunk Word Walk

Lay out the footprints on the ground in a circular walking pattern. Students will walk on the words until someone says "Stop!" Then call on several students (one at a time) to read the words on which they are standing and use them in sentences. Repeat this until every student has had a turn to read one word. Clean up by collecting the feet and storing them in a self-sealing plastic bag.

Variation

Play music while the students are walking on the footprints. Instruct them to freeze when you stop the music. Proceed with the rest of the activity as described above.

cab	wake	jay	stew	pine	cop	buck
crab	snake	clay	lick	vine	hop	truck
tab	ham	spray	kick	spine	mop	bug
lab	jam	tray	pick	king	pop	hug
grab	ram	bed	sick	ring	top	jug
back	yam	fed	tick	wing	core	rug
tack	clam	wed	light	sling	tore	plug
sack	can	sled	tight	swing	shore	gum
pack	fan	led	right	link	store	drum
shack	man	seed	knight	wink	snore	plum
bag	pan	weed	night	sink	cot	hum
rag	van	feed	bill	mink	dot	thumb
wag	bank	reed	gill	stink	pot	bunk
tag	tank	speed	hill	hip	knot	sunk
flag	sank	bell	mill	lip	spot	dunk
mail	drank	fell	pill	rip	out	skunk
jail	Hank	well	swim	sip	scout	trunk
nail	cap	yell	trim	zip	shout	cry
pail	map	shell	brim	cob	trout	fly
sail	nap	nest	slim	sob	sprout	sky
rain	lap	test	Tim	mob	cow	spy
chain	clap	rest	fin	knob	brow	fry
grain	mat	chest	pin	Bob	plow	
train	rat	vest	tin	lock	owl	
brain	bat	blew	grin	rock	bow	
cake	hat	flew	chin	sock	duck	
lake	cat	chew	line	dock	suck	
rake	hay	pew	nine	clock	puck	

Chunk Word Walk (cont.)

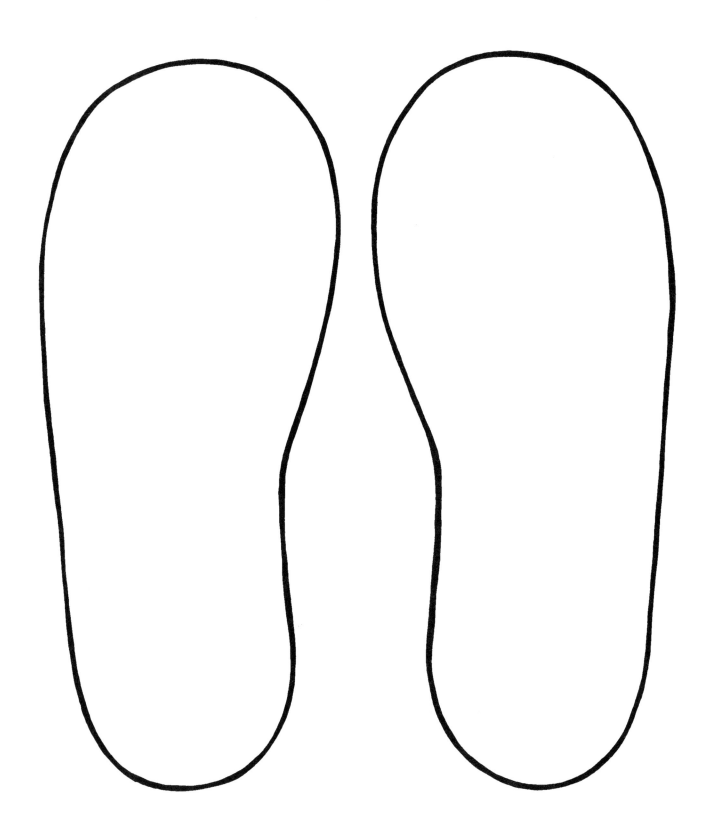

Poetry and Book Resources

Teaching Resource Books That Contain Poetry

Hajdusiewicz, Babs Bell. *Phonics Through Poetry*. Good Year Books. 1998.

Hillstead, Deborah V. and Marjorie V. Fields. *Easy and Irresistible Word Family Poems and Puppets*. Scholastic. 2002.

Moore, Helen H. *A Poem a Day*. Scholastic. 1997.

Schlosser, Kristin. *Thematic Units for Kindergarten*. Scholastic. 1995.

Warren, Jean and Gayle Bittinger. *Toddler Theme-A-Saurus*. Totline Books. 1991.

Anthologies of Poetry

Cole, Joanna. *Anna Banana: 101 Jump-Rope Rhymes*. Scholastic. 1991.

de Paola, Tomie. *Tomie dePaola's Book of Poems*. Putnam. 1988.

de Regniers, Beatrice Schenk. *Sing a Song of Popcorn*. Scholastic. 1990.

Dunn, Sonja. *Crackers and Crumbs*. Heinemann. 1990.

Frank, Josette. *Eloise Wilkin's Poems to Read to the Very Young*. Random House. 1982.

Ghigna, Charles. *Animal Trunk: Silly Poems to Read Aloud*. Harry N. Abrams, Inc. Publishers. 1999.

Prelutsky, Jack. *The Random House Book of Poetry for Children*. Random House. 1983.

Rosen, Michael and Bob Graham. *Poems for the Very Young*. Kingfisher. 1993.

Sendak, Maurice. *Chicken Soup with Rice*. HarperCollins Children's Books. 1990.

Silverstein, Shel. *A Light in the Attic*. Harper Collins. 1996.

Silverstein, Shel. *Where the Sidewalk Ends*. HarperCollins. 2000.

Picture Books With Rhythmic Quality

Barchas, Sarah E. *I Was Walking Down the Road*. Scholastic, Inc. 1975.

Cauley, Lorinda Bryan. *Clap Your Hands*. Penguin. 2001.

Christelow, Eileen. *Five Little Monkeys Jumping on the Bed*. Houghton Mifflin. 1998.

Cronin, Doreen. *Click, Clack, Moo: Cows That Type*. Scholastic. 2001.

Degen, Bruce. *Jamberry*. HarperCollins. 1995.

Hubbard, Patricia. *My Crayons Talk*. Henry Holt and Co. 1999.

Seuss, Dr. *Fox in Socks*. Random House. 1976.

Slate, Joseph. *Miss Bindergarten Gets Ready for Kindergarten*. Scholastic. 1998.

Taback, Simms. *There Was an Old Lady Who Swallowed a Fly*. Scholastic. 1999.

Related Books from Teacher Created Materials

TCM 2757—*Dr. Fry's 1000 Instant Words*

TCM 2763—*Dr. Fry's Picture Nouns*

TCM 2481—*Word Walls Activities*

TCM 2761—*Phonics Patterns by Dr. Fry*

TCM 2762—*Phonics Charts by Dr. Fry*

TCM 3522—*Dr. Fry's Pocket Charts: Effective Ideas and Activities*

TCM 3523—*Dr. Fry's Instant Words Bingo: A Game for Learning Instant Words*